# Take Care of your music Business

PJ KELLY & Associates

# TAKE CARE OF YOUR MUSIC BUSINESS

## *The Legal and Business Aspects You Need to Know to Grow in the Music Industry*

JOHN P. KELLOGG, ESQ.

FOREWORD BY GERALD LEVERT

PJ's Publishing
A Division of PJ KELLY & Associates
Pennsylvania

Published by PJ KELLY & Associates, Bushkill, Pennsylvania 18324.


Library of Congress Cataloging-in-Publication Data

Kellogg, John P.
Take care of your music business/John P. Kellogg
Includes index.
ISBN -0-9675873-0-1

Title: Take Care of Your Music Business

Design by Nighthawk Design
First printing
Manufactured in the United States of America

Illustrator, Khalid Birdsong
Photographer, Mychal Lilly

Take Care of Your Music Business is a PJ's Publishing book, published by PJ KELLY & Associates.

# CONTENTS

# FOREWORD

Gerald Levert

## Moving Forward

We all started out a long time ago. I was a kid about 18 and ready to sign my first contract. I had stars in my eyes and my head was full of living the life of an entertainer like I'd seen my father do while I was growing up. I didn't know much about the business then, but I knew I was getting what a lot of people didn't get—a break! I remember my dad had his attorney review the contract, give me advice and warnings, and stand right beside me while I signed my name on the dotted line!

The attorney was a young man who knew more than I thought he could or should have known and was all about business and music. He was a guy with a little to say about everything. I'd known him for a long time because he had been representing my dad and The O'Jays for a few years by that time (and because a name like Kellogg was a little hard to forget), but I didn't know much about the person or his capabilities.

What I would soon learn about him was that his main objective as an attorney was to protect my rights as an artist for then and for the future, and my dad's rights as an artist and a business for then and the future. He had plans and vision, not only for our success and survival in the intense music world, but also for his law office to grow in order to serve clients based on as much knowledge about the business as he could offer.

We've all been moving forward ever since—through any and all stumbling blocks.

It hasn't been easy. It's been nonstop work, a lot of sacrifices, and years spent making my business grow. From the beginning John has been with me as my attorney and adviser and together we've made a lot of deals happen. When it comes to contracts for co-publishing and writing for and working with people like Patti LaBelle, Barry White, Keith Sweat, Diane Warren, and Anita Baker, John has reminded me that it's about more than a hit song. He lets me know that, before I lend my name or my music and before I appear in commercials or movies, it's got to be business first. He's been there to do his job of drafting and reviewing contracts so I'm protected as well as my company—and to make certain I stay protected and get paid! It's meant growing, developing, and maintaining my business.

In his book, *Take Care of Your Music Business* (TCB), John takes the opportunity to share his legal and business expertise as well as his ideas and he does so with a perspective different than you might expect. The slant he adds is due in part to the fact that he is a unique individual but also because he's an artist in his own right. For the reader, he fuses his passion for artist survival with the knowledge and sincerity (yes, I said sincerity) of a legal mind determined to get the job done—client first. He tempers the weighty business issues with anecdotes about people in the music industry, most of whom he knows and has worked with, others he's read about. His book reminds us that everyone in this business should be well advised. He offers information those of us in the business of making music need to know and the kind of information that keeps everyone strong and professional. Somewhere in the pages of this book, without us actually hearing it, we're reminded that knowledge is power.

In combining his perspectives, John provides material that's the best I've seen yet. There's no denying that good material is on the market but none of it is written by a person who is an artist (when he told me he was with Cameo and had his own band years ago, I couldn't believe it!), has his Juris Doctorate, *and* is a practicing entertainment lawyer with more than fifteen years experience in the music business. When a person like this talks and wants to share advice, I know he's worth listening to.

I'm honored I was asked to write the foreword for John's book. It gives me a chance to say thank you to a man who has been with me through many ups and downs, to a man who had stood by and stood up to any and every situation, whether easy or difficult, whether we agreed or disagreed (yes, we've had those, too). And it gives me a chance to say what I've said to many other entertainers: "Before you sign *anything*, talk to *my* lawyer!"

Gerald Levert
*Recording Artist and CEO, Trevel Production Co., Inc.*

# ACKNOWLEDGMENTS

To my Lord and Savior, Jesus Christ, thank You for the continued health, strength, and the opportunity to share the knowledge I've been able to acquire from the experiences of my life.

To my lovely, talented wife and love of my life, Sandra Jackson. Every day with you is a dream come true.

To my children, Maurice, Andre, John Warren, and Dannielle. I love you. Remember, education is the key. To my sisters, Vivienne Howze and Donna Birdsong, sister- and brother-in-law, Margreat Jackson and Bill Jackson, to my mother- and father-in-law, Pearl and William Kelly Jackson, my aunt and uncle, Carrie and William Ray, and my nieces and nephews, Khalilah, Khalid, Brandon, and Crystal Joy. To Andy Gibson, C.P.A., and President, Trevel Production Co., Inc., my great friend without whom I would not have had the opportunity to represent two of the greatest artists in the world, Gerald Levert and Eddie Levert, Sr. Thank you Eddie Levert, Sr. and Walter Williams, for giving "this kid straight out of law school" the chance to represent the greatest vocal group of all time, The mighty, mighty O'Jays. And to Gerald Levert, my friend, supporter, little brother, and best client. We've still got some more big deals to do!! I love you all.

And finally, I dedicate this book to the memory of my wonderful parents, Ruth W. and Attorney John W. Kellogg.

# INTRODUCTION

A funny thing happened to me on the way to my office recently. While coming out of a major label's office building, I ran into a close acquaintance who also works in the record industry. This person had recently been appointed general manager of a hip-hop production company that was affiliated with the same label I was working with. I asked him how things were going. He looked a little disappointed and said, "Man, one of our major artists just produced and delivered his latest LP. We were anxious to put it out right away, but found there were no written agreements with the songwriters or the producers, and now everybody is fighting over their shares and production credits. Some of these production companies just don't have their business together." I said, "Oh, really! Well, I just happen to be the featured speaker at a series of seminars across the country dealing with that very subject, 'Taking Care of Business for Your Music Production Company—The Legal & Business Aspects You Need to Know to Grow in the Music Industry.'" And he said, "Really? That's great, it's just what these production companies, artists, and songwriters need." I went on to tell him that during the seminars I'd be advising the audiences on business structure, copyrights, and contracts. He said, "That sounds great." Then I said, "You know, you should recommend that I bring the seminar in-house for all the label's production affiliates so they can be schooled on how to really take care of their business." His initial reply, "That sounds fantastic!" was quickly followed by a look of total exasperation and dejection. "But, I really don't think 'they' (the major labels) want them (production companies) to understand *that* much." That's when I knew it was time for me to get the information out to the people in the music business who need it: artists, songwriters, producers, lawyers, and accountants. Before I could commit to the next seminar, I knew I had to write this book.

In this day and age, record companies are primarily the manufacturers and distributors of product and it is their job to contract with production companies to locate, produce, and deliver recordings of talented artists. It is not a mandatory part of their job to educate or offer guidance to the talent. While they may have the experience and resources, in most instances they simply do not have the time to educate each individual act. Therefore, it is in the best interest of all artists, songwriters, and producers to undertake the responsibility of securing the facts and materials needed in order to take care of their music business.

My business is entertainment law and I specialize in music contracts and making them work for the artist. Businesses thrive on contracts, from simple forms that are signed with a cable TV installation to the sixty-five-page tomes that outline a recording artist's rights and obligations to a record company. The objective in my business is to make the fine print in the contract as profitable as it can be for the client. In order to do this, I've sometimes had to fight against the current "status quo," take unprecedented leaps, and step out on faith. This approach has enabled me to learn the intricacies of this business and to be able to share in this book what I deem vital to anyone who has the desire and the talent to be involved in the music industry. It's written from my perspective as an attorney who appreciates the value of the law, as a businessman who knows it's essential to seek assistance in order to succeed, and as an artist who knows the difficulties of putting creative talent on the line.

If, for even a moment, you wonder whether this information is important, you might consider the long list of artists who (after selling millions of albums) have had to file for bankruptcy within the past few years. Mega-hit performers such as M.C. Hammer, Toni Braxton, and the members of TLC and Run DMC are only a few of the many artists who have had their careers altered because they didn't have the right information to grow in the music business. I haven't talked to them but I'm sure each artist would urge anyone interested in being part of the music business to do whatever they can to gain a better understanding of its legal and business aspects. Many artists learned too late about the ramifications of a contract they signed without knowing better, but you don't have to.

Before you go any farther, I have to disclose to you that the information you will gain from this book (although extremely helpful) will not and cannot make you an instant expert in the field of entertainment law or accounting. I also have to tell you that what I impart in these pages is not designed to eliminate the need for you to turn to competent professionals in these areas in order to handle your business properly. Every creative person in this business needs the services of a qualified and experienced lawyer and accountant. What this book is designed to do is to educate you regarding the issues you need to be aware of, and prepare you for more effective communication with such professionals.

This is the book even *I've* been waiting for and the one many people have asked to have. It's about taking care of business in the record industry for today *and* tomorrow. This data, which I've culled from my years of law practice, will give you the edge you need to succeed in this business. I take you through the various business structures under which a music production company can operate to the details of the premier agreements used in this trade (the exclusive recording artist, co-publishing and administration, exclusive songwriter and management agreements) to my epilogue on the past and future of the omnipotent sect of entertainment today. Not only do I present and interpret the contracts, but knowing how important they are in business, I have also underscored the method used to coordinate these agreements. This is done to point out how to maximize the earning potential of each agreement for the benefit of the artist, songwriter, or the music production company owner. And, as this is the day of electronic sampling through the use of keyboards and borrowing from compositions and master recordings, I've included essential advice regarding the protection and exploitation of what I know to be the music industry's most valuable asset: the copyright. Lastly (because ultimately we all have a vested interest), I've incorporated and analyzed statements of the various sources of revenue of the music production company, following the money as it flows through contracts, to the accounts, and into the hands of the people in this business.

I've geared this book to not one, but all the industry players who want to grow in the music business—from the artists to the record company executives.

I've given all I can give within the pages of this book, and now it's your turn.

Let's get down to business.

# 1

# What is a Music Production Company?

## *History, Growth, and Development*

A music production company is a business that is in charge of, or responsible for, the production and delivery of master recordings of songs ready for manufacture and commercial release. A production company may consist of one or more individuals doing business together in a room inside a home, an office building, or someone's basement or garage. It may or may not have a recording studio.

Many times music production companies are like "subcontractors" to the major record label and the major label may rely on the production company to not only locate and discover new artists, but also to nurture and groom these artists' talents.

This is a big change from the way the record companies were run over thirty years ago, when the labels had staff A&R men whose primary job was to find new talent to develop. At the time, the major label would absorb the business overhead expenses of maintaining an office, a recording studio, and a staff of in-house songwriters or producers to develop and direct the recording of the artists in a manner which would create a distinctive style and sound (i.e., Motown Sound, Stax Sound, Sound of Philadelphia). The label would also pay for its lawyers to handle the in-house agreements between staff producers, songwriters, and artists while their accountants would account to the various parties.

As time went on, rock and R&B music became dominant genres. Due to the frequent change of the popular sound and artists who were often singer-songwriters who now wanted to produce their own music, the major labels were not as capable of successfully developing hit artists on an in-house basis. Spurned by necessity, they saw an opportunity to reduce their business overhead expenses and still get the product needed to compete in the market. This was achieved by contracting with the artists' production companies or independent production companies who discovered and produced new talent on an act-by-act basis. Not only did this make the major labels more adept at handling the rapid changes in the marketplace, but it also eliminated the need to pay for the handling of the day-to-day business of contracting and monitoring the activities of producers, songwriters, and artists, which had now shifted to the production companies.

These new production companies, some of which were headed by former major label staff employees, were now fully independent businesses, saddled with the responsibility and expense of forming and staffing an entity, contracting with other producers, songwrit-

**Development of Independent Music Production Company**

**Thirty Years Ago**

*Major Labels*
*Absorbed*
*Business Overhead Expense of paying*
*Lawyers,- Accountants, and*

| Staff Producer | In-House Recording Studio | Staff Songwriters | Staff A&R Representatives |
|---|---|---|---|

## Development of Independent Music Production Company

**Today**

*Major Labels*
*Pay*
*Advances to the*

*Production Company*
*Must Now Absorb*
*Business Overhead Expenses*
*Office, Telephone, Lawyers, Accountants Fees as well as Miscellaneous Expenses*

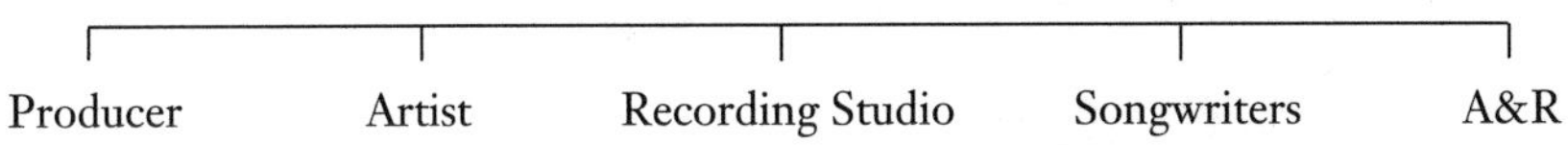

Producer Artist Recording Studio Songwriters A&R

ers, and artists, and even negotiating and monitoring agreements with major record labels for the release of their product.

It has now progressed to the point where there are literally thousands of music production companies. On one CD you might find as many production companies responsible for the CDs tracks as you do the number of tracks on the CD.

This massive growth in the number of music production companies has not only led to opportunities for the new business owners, but has also created a challenge for those businesses to adhere to sound business principles and practices in order to grow and succeed.

2

# The Three Big P's

## *Keys to Success in Today's Music Industry*

I've been known to say that show business is 10% show and 90% business. I applaud you for buying this book and being interested in understanding the 90% business part of the equation, because without that part, the show and the dough will not go on. Even though you know the music, or you know many of the musicians, or you know a lot of the A&R reps who work with talented songwriters, producers, and artists, it won't mean anything if you don't know the legal and business aspects. You may even get that "big hit" but if your lawyer hasn't properly prepared contracts with your clients, artists, producers, and songwriters, you may not be able to continue the relationship so that you can benefit from the second, third, and fourth hits. If your accountant does not properly take care of your business so that you can receive the highest return on your investment in discovering, nurturing, and grooming the next R. Kelly, Jay Z, Shania Twain, or Kirk Franklin, you will definitely not achieve that Berry Gordy, David Geffen, or Russell Simmons type of success you're looking for. If you, the songwriter, artist, or producer, have no understanding of the contract's terms and the effect of those terms on your earning capacity, you, too, might sell millions of CDs, yet end up with nothing.

So, rather than give you the hype and the puff about the parties and the possibility of becoming a millionaire overnight, I want the end result of your time spent reading this book to be the recognition, realization, and application of what I call the three big principles, or the Three Big P's for Success, in today's music industry.

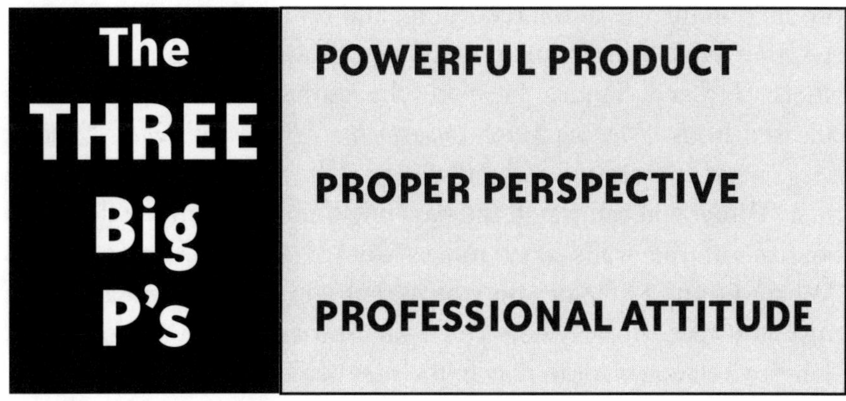


After reading this book you will have gained an understanding of the last two Big P's, but the first Big P—*Powerful Product*—goes far beyond anything that can be stated or discussed in this or any other book. It's what comes from the heart and is laid in the tracks. And because of that, I will deal with this P first.

## POWERFUL PRODUCT

I once heard George Daniels, owner of not just any retail record establishment, but the infamous George's Music Room in Chicago, Illinois, say that music is "memories and emotion."

And he was right. The job of a successful production company is to develop and produce **Powerful Product** that captures, in a song, emotions strong enough to cause memories to last forever. A piece of powerful product has to create with music emotions that are so strong that a remake of the record or song will evoke memories years after its first release. The Fugees' 1996 remake of the hit "Killing Me Softly with Your Song," originally recorded by Roberta Flack many years ago, is an example of that principle. I was driving with my then nine-year-old daughter when this song came on the radio and she started singing it word for word. I thought about the original version, the great sound of Roberta Flack's voice, the full production quality of the recording, and remembered the emotions the song evoked in me many years ago. Powerful product is everywhere. I asked Sandra Jackson, the author of the soon-to-be-released book, *Moving With Love to the Rhythm of Time, "Angie's Song"* what "powerful product" meant to her and she relayed it like this: "When you can watch the bass line build up from the floor and bounce off the walls as it moves toward you in Marvin Gaye's 'What's Going On?,' or you realize that you're rolling on a mellow mist of sweet music when you hear Smokey moan 'Oooh Baby, Baby;' when you want to play in the rain while the Temptations pour down their sunshine and soak you with 'My Girl,' or when Pavoratti's notes breeze along the length of your arms when he whispers out in 'O' Sole Mia,' powerful product has truly moved your life."

Memories and emotion drive this business. Selling memories and emotion is this business and **Powerful Product** is the engine which runs this business! Powerful product is hard to describe, but you know it when you hear it and you know you'll hear it for years to come.

## PROPER PERSPECTIVE

There are two important components to gaining the **Proper Perspective** of doing business as a production company in today's music industry. One component is external and the other is internal.

**Both are critical to the future of your business.** The *external factor*, over which you have no control, is to recognize that the major record labels operate on a very sophisticated and successful level and are out to maximize their value for the benefit of shareholders and the continued success of their business. Repeat that to yourself when you wonder if the record label is interested in making new friends or meeting their bottom line.

This industry generated $38.7 billion in global music sales in 1998, a year in which the merger of Universal/MCA with Polygram reduced what used to be referred to as the "Big Six" record labels to the "Big Five" (Universal/Polygram, EMI, Sony, BMG, and WEA). Most recently, Time Warner Inc. (owner of WEA) proposed a merger with EMI which could further reduce the "Big Five" to the "Big Four." And while total sales of music increased only 60% from 1987 to 1994, the money generated from sales of those units during that same period increased 115%. Over the years, the Big Five have vertically integrated into record distribution and manufacturing concerns, lowering their per unit cost while increasing and maintaining the actual retail selling price of CDs to above $11, drastically improving their bottom line. As you can see in the CD Cost/ Profit Breakdown diagram, the record company's profit portion of the take is nearly $6 per CD. So whether you do business on your own or with the major record labels, it is important to have the proper perspective about the majors' business relationship with the primary provider of music to major record labels, the music production company.

The *internal component* is to understand that when major record labels advance money to music production companies, they are, in essence, funding the start (and hopefully the continuation) of a business which you *do* have control over. It is important to remember that money received for funding the business is not solely for the personal use of the production company owner. It is for defraying the many costs associated with the creation and production of recordings upon which the production company's business is based.

Developing the proper perspective will help you to appreciate

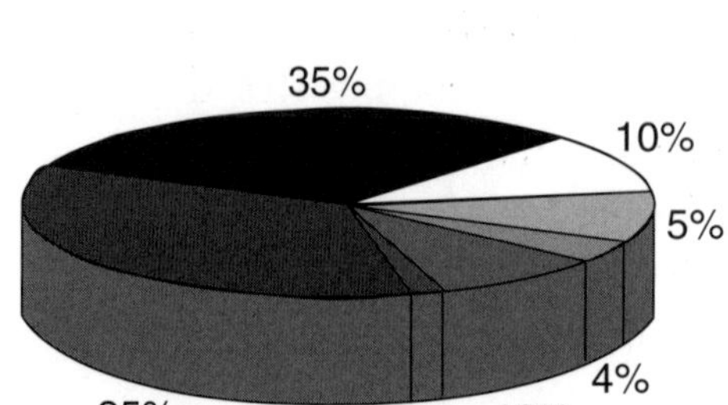

| | | |
|---|---|---|
| **C.D. Retail Price** | | **$15.98** |
| *** Less:** | Production Co. & Artist Royalty | $1.50 (10%) |
| | Manufacturing & Packaging | $ .75 (5%) |
| | Mechanical Royalty | $ .70 (4%) |
| | Distributors Fees | $1.56 (10%) |
| | Union Fee | $ .16 (1%) |
| | Retailer Gross Margin | $5.59 (35%) |
| **Label Profit (Marketing & Overhead)** | | **$5.72 (35%)** |

* These are approximate costs.

money for what it actually is and to put into practice the strategies that should lead to more successful control of your funds. To help you better understand this, I would like to share a theory I have on "When a Million Dollars Ain't a Million Bucks."

There are a lot of people who are attracted to the music industry because of the potential to make "big money." This belief is certainly nurtured by the barrage of stories that appear daily in the news media about the millions of dollars made by a few artists, producers, and songwriters. What these stories usually fail to mention are the costs to operate their businesses. The operating costs are borne primarily by the artists, producers, and songwriters who receive those millions. To put this very essential point in perspective, I think it's important to know "When a Million Dollars Ain't a Million Bucks."

Many times you hear the term "a million bucks" in lottery commercials and, in that context, when we think of lottery winnings, we think of money given with "no strings attached." Everyone knows that the IRS always has its strings attached, even with lottery winnings, but, after that, most people know these "winnings" are free and clear of other strings. Well, a million dollars advanced by a major record label to a music production company has many strings attached (*including* the IRS!).

I have a cousin, Clark Kellogg. He's currently a basketball color analyst for CBS, but he used to be an all-pro forward for the NBAs Indianapolis Pacers (he's on the "big side" of the family). He played in the early 1980s and it was reported in a newspaper at the time, that his yearly salary was $450,000, which is small in comparison to the $100 million multiyear contracts signed by some NBA stars today. After recovering from the fact that my little cousin was making that much money, I decided to calculate the amount of his biweekly check. After doing the calculation over a fifty-two-week year, I concluded that a $17,000 gross check every other week sounded like a pretty decent amount for someone to start building financial security. Even after satisfying Uncle Sam's attached string, a net of $12,000 to $13,000 every two weeks to spend, save, or invest on a personal level still sounded pretty good. And that caused me to think about the difference between salaries paid to athletes and "advances" made to music production companies. It's a comparison of what I call "a million dollars versus a million bucks" and brings up an interesting analogy that best illustrates my theory "When a Million Dollars Ain't a Million Bucks." I hope this analogy helps create the proper perspective of the "million-dollar contract" in the music industry.

**"Man, I just signed a million-dollar contract." The music company production owner, not to be outdone, says, "You too, man? I also just signed a million-dollar contract today." The question is, who has a "million dollars" and who has the "million bucks?"**

Let's say there is an athlete (an NFL football player) and a music production company owner sitting in a bar comparing notes. The football player says, "Man, I just signed a million-dollar contract." The music company production owner, not to be outdone, says, "You too, man? I also just signed a million-dollar contract today." The question is, who has a "million dollars" and who has the "million bucks?"

$1 MILLION BUCKS
TAXES $400,000
AGENT'S FEE $30,000
NET AFTER TAXES $570,000

The athlete makes the "million bucks" in that he has the almighty IRSs string attached, but little else. The salary he earns is just that, a "salary." He doesn't have to pay for his equipment or uniforms; those are supplied by his employer—the team. He doesn't have to pay for his shoes. As a matter of fact, a shoe company will probably pay him handsomely to wear their brand while he's working in the stadium where his games take place, the rent for which is paid by his employer—the team. He receives a sizable per diem for each day's food and incidentals, and his hotel and airfare are all paid for by his employer—the team. You see, the team is the producer of the product, the game, in which the ballplayer is playing. The athlete does not have to bear the expense of creating the product. After taxes he may have approximately $570,000 for personal use over the life of the "million-bucks" contract.

The exact opposite is true in the case of the music production company owner. You see, music production company owners are responsible for creating the product—the master recordings—and when they receive a million dollars from a major label, believe me, it ain't a million bucks. It's a million-dollar advance that is recoupable against future royalties they might earn, and has all kinds of strings attached—the strings of business overhead expenses. The music production company's million dollar contract may also be contingent upon the delivery of four LPs over two years at $250,000 per LP, payable in installments of one-half ($125,000) upon commencement of recording of each LP and $125,000 upon satisfactory delivery of each LP. Just look at the strings attached to the production company owner's "million dollars" as opposed to the athlete's "million bucks." As you can see in the diagram, the production company owner has to pay for office rent, telephone bills, lawyers, accountants, and more, in addition to paying the artist's, producer's, and songwriter's advances and royalties.

With all the expenses of running the production company business, the production company owner may end up with only $200,000 over the life of the "million-dollar" contract *before* personal income taxes. As you can see by the bottom-line comparison

$1
MILLION
DOLLARS
Office Rent
$50,000
Attorney
$50,000
Accountant
$50,000
Telephone
$50,000
$300,000
(4x75,000)
Per LP
Travel
lodging
perdiems
studio
costs
Recording Costs
Artists' ADVANCES
$100,000
4 Artists
at
25,000 each
Taxes
$100,000
Producer/
Musician
ADVANCES
+
Fees
$100,000
4 x $25,000 per LP
$200,000
NET BEFORE
PERSONAL TAXES

with the athlete, the difference is substantial. That's when you know, at least in the music business, "A Million Dollars Ain't a Million Bucks."

Having the proper perspective (while producing your powerful product) of the industry will help you to understand the necessity of conducting your business in conformance with the last Big P—**Professional Attitude.**

## PROFESSIONAL ATTITUDE

The major record label has, as one of its many jobs, the responsibility of advancing hundreds of thousands of dollars to the music production company. As a result, it has to depend on the production company owner to handle his or her company's business in a fair and professional manner. The last thing a major label needs is for the production company to deliver master recordings only to find out, in the middle of the manufacturing process, that a producer, artist, or songwriter has a claim against the production company for failing to properly compensate them. This could occur if the production company fails to properly clear samples, pay recording costs, or obtain the complete rights to the masters. Therefore, it is imperative for you to be educated in the business and hire qualified, experienced professionals to help you carry on your business in a professional and businesslike fashion.

It's also the responsibility of the production company to have a business plan for success so that its employees and artists can feel confident they will be paid in a timely manner and to allow its managers to monitor their performance to ensure that they are working to achieve the company goals. All contracts should be drafted, negotiated, executed, and kept on file for future reference. There should be timely communication of vital information to the company's team members, which is important and crucial to projecting a positive image within the organization. With this type of internal display of "professional attitude," you'll garner respect which will ultimately have a positive effect on your success with the major

**POWERFUL PRODUCT, PROPER PERSPECTIVE, PROFESSIONAL ATTITUDE**

labels and other companies you do business with. These are the principles upon which successful production companies and musical careers should be established and maintained: The Three Big P's. Remember,

These are my keys to starting and growing a successful music production company and musical career.

# 3

# Choosing the Proper Business Structure for Your Production Company

## *Sole Proprietorship*
## *General Partnership*
## *Corporation*
## *Limited Liability Company (LLC)*

In order to start a successful music production company, it is first necessary to choose the proper business structure in which to operate. Keep in mind that the type of business structure that's good for you depends on a number of variables only you are aware of. The structure that's good for one company may not be good for another. After reading about the four recommended structures, make your choice based on *your* particular needs, no one else's.

Sole proprietorships and general partnerships may be what you call "de facto" entities, which means that even though there may be no written organizational document identifying the business as such, the fact that the business exists and has the qualities of either a sole proprietorship or partnership may be enough for it to be legally recognized as one or the other under a state's law.

***Sole Proprietorship.*** A sole proprietorship is an entity owned by an individual, called a sole proprietor. It may be a good way to do business—by yourself! No boss or partners to answer to. You make all the decisions and make all the profit. But, on the flip side, you bear the burden of all blame should things fail. Do you have to be a Mr. or Ms. Know-It-All to pursue success in this form of business? No! If you conduct your business in this manner, you can hire employees or consultants, accountants and lawyers to assist you in the business, provided these individuals have a clear understanding of their role, defined and documented through written agreements or letters of engagement identifying them as "hired help," not co-owners or partners. This is particularly important when dealing with close friends or relatives. It can be very easy for a brother, sister, cousin, or friend to "volunteer" services or money to establish your business. But, unless you have a written agreement clearly defining and limiting their role, they could, over time, consider themselves a co-owner of what you thought was your sole proprietorship. You might feel it's unnecessary to have written agreements with close friends and relatives, but keep in mind that if you don't, they could eventually sue you for an interest in what was once your business. While the sole proprietorship form of business may seem preferable, it also has its risks should the business experience financial difficulty.

A sole proprietor may be held personally liable for claims against his or her business. Suppose you, the sole proprietor, fail to, or are unable to, pay an outstanding business debt. Any of your personal assets held in your name may be seized and liquidated (sold to convert them to cash) to satisfy a judgment rendered against you as the result of a valid claim from a creditor.

As far as taxes are concerned, all profits and losses from your sole proprietorship must be accounted for on your personal tax return.

So, if the expenses exceed the business's income for a particular tax year, your personal taxable income may be reduced accordingly. Of course, should your business show a profit, that profit may increase your taxable income. Thus, the sole proprietorship form of business may be particularly attractive to the new entrepreneur who anticipates investing significant amounts to get the business started and doesn't expect to receive profits from the business the first few years.

**SUMMARY OF SOLE PROPRIETORSHIP**

| | |
|---|---|
| **Limit on Number of Owners:** | One (1). |
| **Management:** | Sole proprietor may manage or employ others (i.e., as employees or consultants) to manage. |
| **Liability of Sole Proprietor:** | Personally liable for claims against the business. |
| **Income Tax Treatment:** | Sole proprietorship's profits or losses are taxed to or deducted from owner's personal income. |

***General Partnership.*** A general partnership is "an agreement between two or more individuals to conduct business for the purpose of making a profit." Does this agreement have to be in writing? No! A court can determine that a partnership exists based on either an express oral agreement of the partners or an implied agreement that is not spoken between the partners, but is manifested by the actions of the partners. For instance, Party A spends time finding talented songwriters, singers, and musicians and coordinating the production of demonstration tapes to shop with a major label. Party B contributes monies to finance the operation and represents to others, with A's knowledge, that he or she is A's partner, an assertion which, at the time, A doesn't dispute. Should success occur and A attempts to deny the existence of a partnership, B may prevail in proving that an "implied" partnership existed, manifested by the parties' actions, and that he or she is entitled to a partnership share.

If you decide to do business with another party on a partnership basis, be sure to have the relationship well defined in the form of a proper written partnership agreement which should, among other things:

- Identify the proper names of the partners and the partnership;
- Define the roles of each partner—specifically, granting or limiting authority of each party to handle various phases of the business;
- Spell out the contribution each party is making to the partnership by way of money or services;
- Define the partners' interest in the partnership's profits and losses and partnership property;
- Denote the method of dissolving the partnership should a partner leave or die; this provision should spell out the method of valuation and payment of a leaving or deceased partner's share;
- Otherwise comply with partnership laws of the state in which you do business.

As with a sole proprietorship, individual partners are each subject to personal liability for partnership debts and, in most states, one partner may be forced to bear the entire debt of the partnership. In other words, a creditor of the partnership may choose to pursue the "deep pocket" partner (the one with the money) for all of the debt of the partnership. That's why it's important to have a written partnership agreement which should, among other things, give the "deep pocket" partner the right to proceed against the other partners for their share of debt should the "deep pocket" partner be "tapped" by a creditor.

A partner is treated just like a sole proprietor for tax purposes. A partner's share of any profit or loss of the partnership must be accounted for on her or his personal income tax returns. It is necessary for an informational partnership schedule to be attached to the partners' tax returns to justify the profit or loss. In this regard, the partnership should apply to the IRS for a TIN (tax identification number) to be used in referencing and filing the informational partnership schedule. A TIN may be obtained by filing a SS-4 form with the IRS, and it is usually necessary to start a bank account in the name of the partnership.

Is a partnership a good form of business for a music production company? Yes, if a properly prepared partnership contract is understood and executed by all partners, doing business as a partnership may be less costly than incorporating, where the ongoing, year-after-year costs of tax preparation, lawyer fees, and other expenses could run into thousands of dollars. The primary drawback of a partnership is that the partners may be subject to personal liability. However, in the case of a new production company, where the potential of liability is low and the probability that start-up expenses that can be written off against personal income is high, the partnership form of business may be the way to go.

### SUMMARY OF GENERAL PARTNERSHIP

| | |
|---|---|
| **Limit on Number of Owners:** | No limit on number of partners. |
| **Management:** | One, some, all, or none of partners may manage the business; however, all of the partners may be subject to liability no matter who manages. |
| **Liability of Partners:** | Each partner may be liable for entire amount of claim against the partnership. |
| **Income Tax Treatment:** | Profit and loss of partnership is "passed through" (i.e., taxed to or deducted from) partner's personal income for federal tax purposes. Profit or loss is prorated among partners. |

***Corporation.*** The corporation is the third form of business structure recommended for the production company. Whereas a sole proprietor or a general partner can be held personally liable for debts and claims against their business, a corporation is deemed, in the eyes of the law, as a third person or entity of its own which can be held liable for debts and claims independent from its owners, the shareholders. Therefore, if actions taken on behalf of a corporation lead to liability, only the corporation's assets, not the shareholders' personal assets, may be used to satisfy the liability. In other words, incorporating creates a corporate shield from liability, protecting the shareholders from being personally liable—*if* the corporation is properly doing business as a corporation.

Some people think that all you have to do to have a valid corporation is to file articles of incorporation with the state in which you're doing business. That's as much a myth as the supposed rule that if you use no more than four (4) bars of another person's song, you can't be sued for copyright infringement. If a corporation is sued and it becomes necessary to prove its validity, you will be expected to produce more than the registered articles of incorporation. In order to prove the existence of an ongoing corporation, a court could demand to see the corporate record book, which should contain by-laws, regulations, proof of notice of annual board and shareholder meetings, minutes of all those meetings, proper election of officers, proof of filing and paying state and federal corporation taxes, and so on. In other words, "articles of incorporation alone do not a corporation make!" If a corporation only files articles and otherwise has not conducted itself as a valid corporation, the court may allow the corporate shield of liability to be pierced and the shareholders may be held personally liable for the corporation's debts or obligations. So, in order to get the full benefits of incorporation, you must also bear the expense of hiring attorneys and accountants to maintain the corporate books and records properly.

While incorporation may shield a shareholder from personal liability, it does result in double taxation. Any profit on the corporate level is taxed at corporate rates and then again on a personal level if and when any of corporate earnings are disbursed to shareholders as payment for services or as a dividend. However, if you meet certain qualifications and make the request within a specified time after incorporation, the IRS allows you to elect subchapter S status. This special tax designation status allows the corporation's shareholders to be treated like partners for tax purposes. The corporation pays no corporate tax on its profit. Instead, the corporation's profit is attributed to the shareholders' personal incomes, according to their ownership interests, and taxed accordingly. This election is recommended to newly formed small corporations which expect losses in the first few years.

### IRS SUBCHAPTER S STATUS

**Purpose:** Allows corporations with few shareholders to whom most of the corporation income is distributed, the ability to be treated as if it were a partnership for income tax purposes, while retaining the corporate advantage of limited liability.

**Qualifications:** In most states, less than thirty-five (35) shareholders who must, in most cases, be individuals (not other corporations or partnerships); S-corporation may have no more than one class of stock.

Most states allow corporations to elect to be "close corporations." Close corporations (see chart, p. 26) usually have fewer than twenty to thirty shareholders and are allowed to conduct business on a less

### CLOSE CORPORATION

**Purpose:** Allows small corporation (where stock is held by a few individuals) the ability to manage its affairs on a less formal basis and restrict the transfer of shares to existing shareholders.

**Qualifications:** All shareholders must assent to terms of a close corporation agreement in writing. The close corporation agreement should, at least, contain provisions which:

Provide for management of the close corporation.

- possibly eliminating the board of directors entirely
- delegating authority to directors, shareholders, officers, or other persons

Specify voting requirements for action by the close corporation.

- approval of corporate action by a certain number of shareholders

Provide for corporate distribution of profit.

- when dividends declared and/or profits shared

Restrict issuance or transfer of shares.

- limit transfer of shares to close corporation shareholders

---

## SUMMARY OF CORPORATION

| | |
|---|---|
| **Limit on Number of Owners:** | None, unless owners desire to elect subchapter S or close corporation status. |
| **Liability of Shareholders:** | Individual shareholders are not held personally liable; corporation's liability is limited to corporation assets. |
| **Income Tax Treatment:** | Corporation must file and pay corporate taxes. Shareholders who receive dividends or other income from the corporation must include such income in their personal income for tax purposes. (Double taxation—corporation pays tax; shareholder pays tax.) |
| **Management:** | Unless under close corporation qualification and election, the corporation is regulated by state statutes requiring formal procedures for conducting the business. |

formal basis than a regular corporation. Close corporations restrict the unfettered trading of shares by requiring shareholders to first offer to sell their shares to other existing shareholders.

The close corporation record book should contain a close corporation agreement, which should:(a) identify the officers; (b) delegate duties; and (c) outline the decision-making process, as well as the method of transferring shares between shareholders. Close corporation designation eases the burden of formalization and creates a mechanism allowing original shareholders to maintain control.

***Limited Liability Company (LLC).*** The fourth form of recommended business entity, the limited liability company (LLC), has just emerged and been approved by most states within the past few years. In some circumstances, the limited liability company may combine the best features of a partnership and a corporation. The owners of an LLC are called "members," rather than shareholders (as in corporations) or partners (as in partnerships). One or more persons may form this type of entity, and by doing so, may limit their liability, as with a Corporation, and receive the favorable tax aspects of doing business as a Partnership. In most instances, an LLC member may not be held personally liable for obligations of the entity.

**SUMMARY OF LIMITED LIABILITY COMPANY (LLC)**

| | |
|---|---|
| **Limit on Number of Owners:** | One or more depending on state law. |
| **Liability of Members:** | In most instances members will not be personally liable; the liability is limited to LLC assets. |
| **Income Tax Treatment:** | Profit and loss "passed through" to members in shares determined by members. |
| **Management:** | All, one, or none of members may manage. Professional manager may be hired. |

LLCs are treated the same as a partnership for tax purposes. All profit and losses of the LLC are apportioned and passed through to the members' personal incomes for taxing or deduction purposes.

In order to form an LLC, most states require the filing of a simple document, referred to as articles of organization. In all instances, in addition to the articles of organization, it is advisable to have an "operating agreement" between the members which, much like a partnership agreement, sets forth the rights, duties, and responsibilities of the LLCs members and/or managers. The primary drawback of this form of entity is its recent development. It is still unclear how these entities will be treated when claims arise in states outside the LLCs state of origination. However, due to the significant advantages and further proliferation of this form of business in many states, these disadvantages may soon disappear.

4

# The Across the Board Deal

## *How to Maximize Income for Your Production Company*

I'm sure when most of you looked at this book's table of contents, you wondered what an "across the board deal" was. It is the contractual method, sometimes referred to as the blessed trinity of contracts, where a manager or production company signs an artist for management, production, and publishing. It became a popular way to sign artists in the 1970s when managers, who spent a great deal of money to finance the recording, wardrobe, grooming, and sometimes living expenses of artists, sought a way to participate in as many incoming producing activities of artists as possible in order to recoup their investment as quickly as possible. Currently most artists' lawyers would advise their clients not to enter into such agreements because of the inherent potential of conflict of interest caused by managers putting their interest before those of the artist. This can result in the manager "double dipping" or profiting twice—from producing the artist's recordings, *and* publishing the artist's compositions and commissioning the advances and royalties due the artist from these activities. Artist managers initiated this practice years ago, and since then many production companies have adopted it; they sign artists to record demos in order to seek label deals and their principals establish related management companies or divisions to handle the affairs of their artists. While most artists' attorneys may not recommend that their clients enter into this type of arrangement, some production company lawyers still see it as the best way to maximize the revenue potential of an artist to the production company. While I can understand the artist's attorney not wanting a client to enter into this type of arrangement, in certain cases, where the production company is properly run by individuals with the expertise to properly market and promote the acts' recordings, publishing interests, and live performances to a particular genre, an artist may be best served by entering such agreements.

In my experience, most new artists signed to production companies rely on the companies to not only record them, but also to handle various aspects of their business that they may be unfamiliar with. So, if a production company signs a new artist to a recording agreement, it is probable that the artist will also need the company's help and assistance in other areas, such as developing a stage show or arranging the engagement of a booking agent to secure performance dates. If the artist is also a songwriter or has the potential to become a songwriter, he or she may also rely on the production company to do such things as file copyrights, place songs with other artists, and collect any royalties due the artist from the exploitation of his or her compositions.

If your production company has this type of relationship with one of its artists, you may already have an "across the board" relationship. The next step is to convert this relationship into an agreement, reduced to writing in order to clarify the specific terms of the relationship.

This method of signing and working with (and on behalf of) the artist in multiple capacities may also result in the production company maximizing the return on its investment in the artist's career.

If the production company sells the artist's records independently or through a major label, the value of the artist's copyrights will be enhanced. The exposure the artist receives from radio play of the records may also result in him or her receiving more requests for paid live performance dates. In other words, the artist may receive multiple benefits from the production company choosing to record the artist. So, why shouldn't the production company be able to share in the other sources of revenue, such as publishing royalties and live performance fees generated by the artists? Well, with an across the board deal, the production company can, if certain guidelines are adhered to.

**First, the production company must decide whether the increased responsibility which comes along with a commitment to provide these additional services to the artist is worth the time and headache.**

First, the production company must decide whether the increased responsibility which comes along with a commitment to provide these additional services to the artist is worth the time and headache. As we will discuss in the review of the management agreement, the management business can be a very lonely, time-consuming, and aggravating business with little reward, unless and until the artist has achieved a significant amount of success.

Administering the copyrights of the artist is also very complicated and tedious work that can cause a production company owner to wonder: Is it worth the time and headache? Yes! Because, as you'll read in my chapter on copyright principles, the copyright is the most valuable asset in the music business. The production company owner must realize that the music industry is a hit or miss business. I once heard someone say, "You can't make a living in the music business, you can only make a killing! The object is to put as many killings together as you can." I disagree with this saying. There are certainly a number of ways to make a decent living in the music business. However, investing time and money in this business certainly involves a significant amount of risk. The chances of failure are great, but, if your artists hit the top of the charts, selling out records, performances, and merchandise, you certainly want to be in a position to participate in as many streams of revenue as possible.

In an across the board deal, the production company concurrently signs the artist to an exclusive recording artist agreement, a co-publishing and administration agreement, an exclusive songwriter agreement, and a management agreement. (The agreements will be discussed and analyzed through the remainder of this book.)

As noted in the following diagram, I recommend using different names for the production company's publishing and management operations for purposes of clarifying each operation's function, as well as creating separate accounting systems for each.

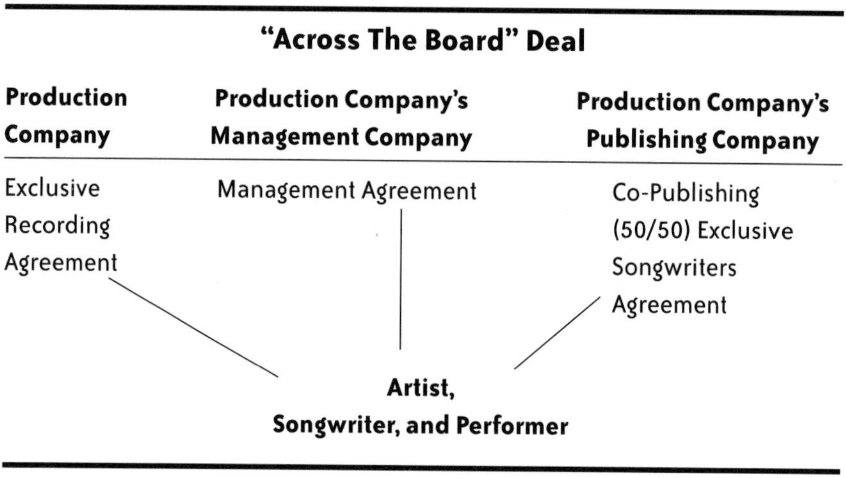

**"Across The Board" Deal**

| **Production Company** | **Production Company's Management Company** | **Production Company's Publishing Company** |
|---|---|---|
| Exclusive Recording Agreement | Management Agreement | Co-Publishing (50/50) Exclusive Songwriters Agreement |

**Artist, Songwriter, and Performer**

Also, in order to make this type of relationship stand up under a challenge in court, it is important to adhere to a few rules to counter an artist's challenge that the production company's involvement on so many levels is overreaching, and otherwise too burdensome to the artist and may, therefore, be deemed a breach of the fiduciary duty the production company's management company owes to the artist.

First, make sure that the agreements run concurrently and are coterminous, so that when one contract ends, they all end. Second, the management agreement should specify that no management commission is taken on earnings due the artist from the production company or publishing company. Third, the production company should co-publish, on a 50–50 basis, the artist's copyrights under the terms of a co-publishing and administration contract. If the production company attempts to take 100% of the artist's copyright interests or takes a management commission on the artist's earnings made pursuant to an agreement with the production company or its other affiliates, the validity of the across the board deal may be jeopardized. In other words, the production company's management division may not take a commission on the artist's advances or royalties that are due the artist from the management company's production affiliate. The same is true of advances and royalties due the artist from the production company's publishing affiliate.

In conclusion, although the across the board deal may present a challenge to the production company, it is its best hope of maximizing its return on investing in the development of an artist's career. The artist, on the other hand, must carefully evaluate the personnel and structure of a production company that presents it with a set of "across the board" agreements. If the artist recognizes a "weak link" in the production, publishing, or management "chain" of the company proposing the deal, he or she should attempt to negotiate separate agreements upon more favorable terms with only the divisions of the company that are determined to be capable to do a credible job of advancing their career.

5

# Contracts and Accounting Statements

## *Introduction*

Now it's time to begin the review of the contracts, samples of which follow.

A contract is a binding agreement between two or more parties and, depending upon a number of factors such as the subject matter of the contract, may be verbal or written. In the music business, it is advisable for all your agreements to be in writing. I must emphasize that the sample contracts and accountings that follow are exactly that—samples. In fact, I disagree with many provisions in some of them, but included them here to point out these deficiencies. In other words, don't consider these "standard contracts." During my years of practice, I have drafted, altered, and negotiated hundreds of contracts. What never ceases to amaze me is how they are all different in some form or fashion. One of the first things professors in law school tell you is how dynamic and ever-changing the field of law is. And were they right? You bet! There may be a few "boiler plate" provisions in every contract, but minor alterations could change the meaning entirely. There is no such thing as standard in today's business. The business is changing so rapidly that a contract that may have been adequate six months ago may be outdated today. Therefore, while these samples serve as a basis for discussion, they are, by no means, recommended for a company or client's specific use, without proper review and revision by an experienced, qualified professional.

*Exclusive recording*, *songwriter*, *co-publishing* and *administration*, and *management* contracts follow. The actual contract is on the left side of the page with my comments on the right side of page. Make sure you read the *entire* contract to get a feel for the language of industry terms and contractual provisions. The comments I've made break down the legalese for you and offer some key hints to understanding and improving some of the provisions.

The statement of recording, copyright, and management earnings is designed to help you see how the money, committed to in the contracts, flows through these contracts to the accounting statements. The contractual provisions related to the accounting entries are indicated for your reference. The analysis following the statement is designed to help you see how the contract serves as the faucet, wherein each contract provision acts as a handle, turning on, or in many cases, closing the valves, through which the money flows to the production company, artist, and songwriter.

6

# Exclusive Recording Artist Contract

## *Analysis of Artist/Production Company Agreement*

**CONTRACT**

**Exclusive Recording Artist Agreement with Production Company**

AGREEMENT made and entered into ____________, by and between:

[Individual Group Member's Names], jointly and individually and collectively professionally known as "[Group Name]" ("Artist")

and

[Production Company's Name] ("Company").

1. (a) Company hereby engages Artist's exclusive services as a recording artist in connection

**ANALYSIS**

**Analysis of Artist/Production Company Agreement**

1.(a) In the not too distant past, the term of what was considered a "Standard Recording Agreement"

## CONTRACT

**with the production of records during the Term throughout the Territory, with choice of material recorded and time and place of recording to each be subject to Artist and Company's mutual approval provided; however, if there is a dispute between Artist and Company, Company's decision shall prevail. The first Contract Period of the Term shall be for a period of the later of (a) Twelve (12) months which will commence as of the date above; or (b) Nine (9) months after the date on which Artist's recording commitment is fulfilled for such first Contract Period. Company will have seven (7) separate and consecutive options, each to renew the Term upon the same terms and conditions applicable to the first Contract Period for additional Contract Periods (such additional Contract Periods will sometimes hereinafter be called "Option Periods"). Each Option Period will run consecutively and will automatically commence at the expiration of the previous Contract Period, unless Company advises Artist of Company's intention not to exercise its option to extend the Term at any time prior to the expiration of the applicable Contract Period. Each Contract Period will not expire until the Option Date for such Contract Period unless Company advises Artist to the contrary. The Option Date for a particular Contract Period will be the later of (a) Twelve (12) months from the com-**

## ANALYSIS

was one year with four one year options which sounded good in theory, but did not work in fact. By that I mean, while the contract was for one year, the recording commitment was for usually one LP, with the record company having the option of requesting one (1) additional LP per contract year. If the record company exercised the option for the additional LP, the contract year would be extended for a certain period of time (usually 6–9 months) following the delivery of the additional LP. This could cause artists to mistakenly think their contracts were for five years (one year with four one year options), when actually, as a result of other small print provisions in the contract, the record company was allowed to extend contracts up to 10 years or longer. It's been a very long time since artists would record (and companies would release) two LPs per year. Therefore, most contracts are now drafted so that the term is based on the time it takes to record an LP which is a period of either twelve (12) months from commencement of the term or seven (7) months following the date of delivery of the LP.

This contract states that options are automatically exercised unless the production company advises the artist to the contrary. Provisions such as these have been stricken down by courts on the basis that it makes the term indefinite. The production company is usually required to give notice of exercise of the option within 30–90 days prior to the end of each period.

**CONTRACT**

**mencement of the applicable period; or (b) Nine (9) months after the date on which Artist's recording commitment is fulfilled for such Contract Period.**

**(b) Artist acknowledges that Company has entered into a Distribution Agreement with [Distributor's Name] ("Distributor") (the "Distribution Agreement") for the distribution of records hereunder. In the event the Distribution Agreement or any successor Distribution Agreement entered into by Company with another Distributor for the distribution of records hereunder (a "Successor Distribution Agreement") contains any grant of rights for Artist's exclusive recording services which provide for additional rights to the benefit of the Distributor which are beyond and greater than the grant of rights and terms and conditions of this Agreement, then the terms and conditions of the Distribution Agreement or any such Successor Distribution Agreement shall control and apply (including, without limitation the duration of the term and the number of masters to be recorded) and Artist's execution of the standard inducement letter which Distributor or such other Distributor requires Artist to execute will further confirm Artist's agreement to be bound thereby. In this connection, Company shall apprise Artist of all relevant terms and conditions of the Distribution Agreement or Successor Distribu-**

**ANALYSIS**

1.(b) This provision acts as an acknowledgement of a distribution agreement which is inserted if the production company has entered into a distribution contract with a major label. As I mentioned earlier when discussing the Three Big P's, the Big Five are giant record distributors. Many production companies desire relationships with them because of their vast distribution, marketing and manufacturing networks. This provision states that if the production company's Distribution Agreement provides a grant of rights for the artist services greater than those outlined in this contract, the Distribution Agreement shall control and apply (i.e., number of Masters, duration of term, etc.). The production company is also obligated to inform the artist if that is the case and what specific terms may be affected, (i.e., while this contract is for a maximum of six (6) LPs, if the contract between the production company and the distributor is for a maximum of eight (8) LPs, then this contract will also be for eight (8) LPs).

**CONTRACT**

**tion Agreement. Artist shall execute all documents, confirmations or assents which Distributor or any such other Distributor deems necessary to be executed by Artist. Notwithstanding the foregoing, nothing in this subparagraph (1)(b) shall operate so as to entitle Artist to share in any recording funds or other advances paid to Company, unless expressly set forth herein.**

**2. (a) All recording costs incurred in connection with any recordings made, in whole or in part, during the Term and any monies incurred by Company in the promotion and marketing of records embodying Artist's performances as well as any monies for any reason paid by Company to or on Artist's behalf will be fully recoupable from any and all royalties at any time payable to Artist. All masters will be subject to approval by Company as commercially satisfactory for commercial release, and will be Company's sole property in perpetuity throughout the Territory free from any claims whatsoever by Artist or any person or party deriving any interest from Artist. Without limiting the foregoing, Company and its designees will have the perpetual and exclusive right throughout the Territory to: (i) manufacture, distribute, exploit and publicly perform Records or other reproductions embodying all or any part of any of the masters by any method (including, without limitation, phonograph records,**

**ANALYSIS**

2.(a) All recording costs in connection with any records and any monies incurred by the company in the promotion and marketing of records are fully recoupable from any and all royalties payable to artist. This means the costs of recording, arranging, traveling, meals, lodging, session musicians, etc., are all recouped from the artist's royalties. Prior to the early eighties, the costs of marketing and promotion were not costs recoupable from the artist's royalties. However, with the rise of independent promotion and video costs, most record companies inserted provisions in their contracts making at least fifty percent (50%) of these costs recoupable. A provision such as the one contained in this contract, making one hundred percent (100%) of these costs recoupable is unusual and clearly excessive considering the expensive costs of producing videos, which range from $100,000 to $1,000,000 per video and $100,000 per single in independent promotion costs.

The artist grants to the record company the exclusive rights to manufacture, and exploit the recordings, by

**CONTRACT**

**cassette tapes, compact discs and digital audio tape), (ii) to sell, lease, license, exploit, transfer or otherwise deal in or alter the same under any trademarks, trade names and labels; and (iii) to obtain copyrights and renewals thereof in all sound recordings recorded by Artist during the Term, in Company's name as owner and employer-for-hire of such sound recordings.**

**(b) Company or the Distributor shall pay all union scale payments required to be made to Artist in connection with the masters, all costs of musicians and other personnel (which have been specifically approved by Company) incurred in the recording of the masters, and all other costs required to be paid by Company or the Distributor pursuant to any applicable law or collective bargaining agreement between Company or Distributor and any union representing persons who have rendered services in connection with the masters. The prepayment of session union scale as provided in the applicable union codes and pension benefits paid on Artist's behalf by Company or Distributor to any such union shall be advances against and recoupable from any royalties becoming payable to Artist under this Agreement. Artist shall complete any documentation required by the applicable union.**

**ANALYSIS**

any method, under any names and trademarks, and obtain copyright and renewals in the company's name as owner, or on an employer for hire basis. This means that the artist transfers all of his or her rights in the recordings to the record company. So, pursuant to this provision, the record company, not the artist, owns the right to license and get paid, in the first instance, for the subsequent use of the recordings as a sample in another record.

(b) Union scale payments to musicians and/or vocalists for sessions are all recoupable as recording costs. Session payments for the artist, should be paid through the appropriate union (i.e., American Federation of Musicians (AFM) or American Federation of Television and Radio Artists (AFTRA). Payment of annual dues and session rates are requirements that are generally ignored by many artist and production companies. However, if an artist receives a certain amount of income from union sessions within a one-year period, he or she may be entitled to important union benefits such as health insurance and pension plans. The artist, who must pay annual dues to the union should require the production company to fill out the proper paperwork and make session payments on their behalf to the union. The union then records the earnings for the artist and pays out the proper fees to the artist. Many production companies object to this procedure because, in addition to having to pay union scale rates for the artist, they must pay

**CONTRACT**

**3. All masters recorded under this Agreement shall consist of Artist's newly recorded studio performances of selections selected and approved by Company and not previously recorded by Artist. Fulfillment of Artist's recording commitment for each Contract Period hereof will consist of delivery to Company of the following: (a) fully mixed, equalized, edited and sequenced master(s), technically and commercially satisfactory to Company in Company's reasonable business judgment, for Company's manufacture and sale of records, clearly marked to identify Artist as the recording artist, the title(s) of the composition(s), recording date(s) and all original and duplicate Masters of the material recorded; (b) all "label copy", typewritten in a form satisfactory to Company, listing the composer, publisher(s), administrator(s), performing rights society(ies) and each master's running time; (c) all "jacket copy" listing the sequence of the master(s), and all technical and artistic credits; (d) the lyrics for each composition embodied on a master, if any and (e) all required licenses and consents. The date of delivery of all the aforementioned items will be the date of fulfillment of Artist's recording commitment for such Contract Period. Upon the request of Company, Artist shall re-record any se-**

**ANALYSIS**

an additional percentage, usually 10-11% of total session fees to the union Health & Welfare plans, for the artist's pension and health benefits.

3. The requirements for delivery of an LP include: fully mixed, sequenced masters, technically and commercially satisfactory in the production company's judgment; label copy, a listing of all publisher information, running times, artistic credits, lyrics of each composition, all recorded licenses and consents. In order to establish a set delivery date, the artist should gather all the required information and include such information in a letter sent certified to the production company. The date of receipt by the production company of all these is deemed the delivery date which is important in determining the term of the contract.

| CONTRACT | ANALYSIS |
|---|---|
| lection until a technically and commercially satisfactory master shall have been obtained. Only masters delivered in full compliance with the provisions of this Agreement shall be applied in fulfillment of Artist's recording and delivery obligation and no payments shall be made to Artist in connection with any masters which are not in full compliance. | |
| 4. (a) During the first Contract Period, Artist shall record and deliver to Company masters the equivalent in playing time of one (1) LP ("minimum recording commitment"). (b) During each Option Period, Artist shall record and deliver to Company masters the equivalent in playing time of one (1) LP ("minimum recording commitment"). (c) The first LP required to be delivered during the Initial Period or any Option Period shall be delivered to Company within three (3) months following commencement of the applicable Period. It is understood that Artist shall not deliver any LP within six (6) months from the date of delivery of a prior LP. | 4. The recording commitment for the first contract period are the masters equivalent in playing time of one (1) LP. The first LP is required to be delivered within three (3) months of commencement of the term, provided no delivery of an LP is made within six (6) months after a prior LP delivery. This type of provision was one of the main issues in the dispute between Warner Brothers Records and Prince. Prince, a remarkable artist, who can probably record the equivalent of ten (10) LPs per year, disagreed with Warner's policy of accepting delivery of only one (1) LP per year, which significantly extended the term of his contract. Warner and Prince settled the dispute and the contract was terminated in the mid-nineties, allowing Prince to release his music independently according to his own release schedule. |
| (d) The masters comprising each LP required to be recorded and delivered hereunder shall hereinafter sometimes be referred to as the "First LP", the "Second | |

**CONTRACT**

**LP", the "Third LP", the "Fourth LP", the "Fifth LP", the "Sixth LP", the "Seventh LP", and the "Eighth LP", etc. respectively, in the order in which same are accepted by Company hereunder.**

**5. (a) (i) Company and any licensee or designee of Company shall have the right and may grant to others the right to reproduce, print, publish or disseminate in any medium, Artist's name(s) and Artist's portraits, pictures and likenesses in connection with the exploitation of master recordings made under this Agreement (including, without limitation, all professional, group and other assumed or fictitious names now or hereafter used by Artist), and biographical material concerning Artist as news or information for the purposes of trade, or for advertising purposes. Artist hereby grants to Company the right to use Artist's names, portraits, pictures, likenesses and biographical material in connection with the sale, marketing and exploitation of the master recordings hereunder and all merchandise of any kind. During the Term of this Agreement, Artist shall not authorize any party other than Company to use said name(s) and likenesses (or any professional, group, or other assumed or fictitious name used by Artist) in any manner. During the Term hereof, Company shall have the right to refer to Artist as Company's exclusive recording artist. Artist shall use its best efforts to cause Artist to be**

**ANALYSIS**

5.(a) This provision grants the right to publicize the artist's name, picture and likeness for purposes of trade or advertising for exploitation of the masters and all merchandise of any kind. Just ask Maurice Starr, whose production company signed New Kids on the Block (NKOTB), about the value of this right. Mr. Starr made millions in the merchandising of NKOTB dolls, pins, caps, and T-shirts. Is this an important right? Absolutely! Does it mean a lot of money to the production company in every instance? No! But in particular cases involving successful groups like Boys II Men, Megadeth, or T.L.C., merchandising revenues can be substantial. Are production companies willing to negotiate this provision? They probably will. It depends on the leverage of the act. Production companies that demand to participate in merchandising are usually willing to share up to 50% of the net profits generated from the sale of the merchandise.

| CONTRACT | ANALYSIS |
|---|---|
| similarly billed in all of Artist's endeavors in the entertainment industry. | |
| (ii) Artist shall be available from time to time to appear for photography, poster and cover art and the like, under the reasonable direction of Company or its nominees, and to appear for interviews with representatives of the communications media and Company's publicity personnel. Artist shall not be entitled to any compensation for such services, except as may be required by any applicable union agreement; provided, however, that if Artist is required to travel outside of a fifty (50) mile radius of Artist's place of residence, Company or the Distributor shall reimburse Artist for Artist's reasonable travel and living expenses incurred by Artist in connection with such services rendered at Company's direction as provided herein pursuant to a budget approved in advance by Company in writing. | |
| (b) (i) Artist hereby grants to Company the exclusive right during the Term hereof and throughout the Territory to use and/or sublicense to others the use of Artist name(s) (both real and professional), logotype, likeness and facsimile signature for merchandizing and other commercial purposes (whether or not such merchandising and commercial | 5.(b) This provision states that if the artist is a group, the group name shall be owned by the production company. This is a very interesting concept which may, depending on the circumstances, lead to the leader of the group hiring the other "group members" as employees for purposes of providing their services for recording and performing. Under this pro- |

**CONTRACT**

**purposes are related to the manufacture and sale of records) in connection with the sale (whether through "Flyers", "bouncebacks" and similar Album inserts, or otherwise) of t-shirts and other apparel, poster, stickers and novelties and any other items ("Merchandising Rights").**

**(ii) Artist hereby agrees that the trademark and servicemark "[Group Name]" (the "Mark") shall be prominently displayed and be utilized at all times in connection with all entertainment services which are rendered by Artist during the Term. Such Mark is and will continue to be Company's sole and exclusive property and Artist warrants and represents that there are and will be no competing claims with respect to Company's right to use or authorize the use of that Mark in all areas of the entertainment industry. During the Term, Company may cause a search to be instituted to determine whether there have been any third party uses for such Mark in connection with records and/or entertainment services. In this connection, with respect to each such search, Company may expend up to Six Hundred Dollars ($600.00), which shall be deemed an advance against and recoupable from all royalties becoming payable to Artist under this or any other agreement. If the aforesaid search indicates that the Mark should not be so used, Com-**

**ANALYSIS**

vision, group members may not be able to claim an ownership interest in the group name. This concept is not new, it started in the fifties with such groups as The Drifters and continued during the 80s funk band era. During that time, many self-contained groups, such as, Earth, Wind, and Fire, Cameo, Funkadelic, Chic, and Wild Cherry, had leaders (in most instances, the group's producers) who might execute a recording contract, as an individual, promising to deliver recordings of a group using the talents of unsigned "group members" whom they could change at will. Many of the leaders would exploit the talents of the "group members" under the terms of oral agreements. These agreements were usually separate from, and totally different from the recording contract, particularly in regard to compensation. The Temptations' motto, "Temptations Forever," is a testament to this concept. The name and the group, The Temptations, has lived on through many changes in group members. From the perspective of the production company, it is a stroke of genius. It allows the production company to maintain the ownership interest in the group name thereby allowing it to replace individual group members at will. One of my motivations for becoming a lawyer stemmed from my experience as a "group member" of Cameo. While I recorded and performed with the group I had no written agreement with the group's leader or the record company.

**CONTRACT**

**pany and Artist shall mutually agree upon a substitute Mark. Artist will not, during the Term, alter the Mark under which Artist renders professional services as a performer and recording artist without Company's prior written consent.**

**(iii) Company agrees to credit to Artist's royalty account with Fifty Percent (50%) of the net income actually received in hand by Company (as opposed to Company's licensees, agents or other representatives) from the exploitation of Merchandising Rights hereunder. For the purposes hereof "net income" shall mean gross income derived directly from the exploitation of such Merchandising Rights, which has actually been received in hand by Company (as opposed to Company's licensees, agents and other representatives) less direct expenses actually incurred by Company relative thereto, including, but not limited to: (i) costs of collection; (ii) commissions and/or royalties payable to third parties; (iii) cost of manufacture and design; (iv) costs of packing, shipping, storing, postage and insurance; and (v) advertising and promotion expenses.**

**6. Artist acknowledges that the sale of records is speculative and agrees that the judgment of Company with regard to any matter affecting the sale, distribution and exploitation of such records shall be binding and conclusive upon Artist. Nothing contained in this**

**ANALYSIS**

I was only told by the group leader how much I would be paid per week. I had no idea how much the group leader, who was also the group's producer, was making from the record company or how much was being paid by promoters for the group's live performance. But most importantly, at that time, I had no right to the group name. I'll discuss newer developments in the law regarding rights to group names later in the book.

**CONTRACT**

**Agreement shall obligate Company to make, sell, license, or distribute records manufactured from masters subject hereto.**

**7. Company shall pay Artist the following sums ("Advance") which shall be advances against and recoupable by Company out of all royalties (excluding mechanical royalties) becoming payable to Artist pursuant to this or any other agreement.**

**(a) With respect to the First LP, Company shall pay Artist the sum of Twenty Thousand Dollars ($20,000.00) as follows:**

**(i) Ten Thousand Dollars ($10,000.00) promptly following the full execution of this Agreement; and**

**(ii) Ten Thousand Dollars ($10,000.00) upon delivery and Company's acceptance of the masters comprising the First LP.**

**(b) With respect to each subsequent LP required to be delivered hereunder, Company shall pay the Artist the following Advances:**

**(i) With respect to the Second LP, if any, the Advance shall be the greater of:**

**(A) the applicable "Base Advance" set forth in subparagraph 7(d) hereof, or**

**ANALYSIS**

7. This is one of the most important clauses for both the production company and the artist. One of the production company's main concerns is the amount of money it has to advance to the artist to record an album. It is also concerned about the additional money it has to pay to produce and market a great record. Of course, the artist wants to be advanced as much money as possible. While it is not unusual for a new Rap or R&B artist to receive an advance of between $25,000 to $50,000 for their first album for a major label, gospel artists advances have historically been lower. However, with the meteoric rise in success of such gospel acts as Kirk Franklin, I anticipate the bar to be soon raised in regards to initial advances paid to some gospel artists. In this contract, the artist is to receive an advance of $20,000 for the 1st LP with advances for subsequent LPs based on a formula. The formula requires the payment of the greater of the minimum advance, which for instance in the case of the 2nd and the 3rd is $15,000, or 10% of the net earned royalties in respect of sales of the 1st LP, up to a maximum of $30,000. Any "min/max" formula (as this type of calculation for advances is called in the industry), which requires payment of anything less than 66% of the prior LPs royalties, is, in my

**CONTRACT**

**(B) an amount which is the equivalent of ten percent (10%) of the net earned royalties in respect of sales of royalty bearing units through normal retailer channels in the United States of the First LP.**

**(ii) With respect to the Third LP, if any, and each subsequent LP required to be recorded and delivered hereunder, the Advance Recording Fund shall be the greater of:**

**(A) the applicable "Base Advance" set forth in subparagraph 7(d) hereof, or**

**(B) an amount which is the equivalent of ten percent (10%) of the average of the net earned royalties in respect of sales of royalty bearing units through normal retailer channels in the United States of the two (2) immediately preceding LPs required to be recorded and delivered hereunder.**

**(c) For the purposes of making the computations under subparagraphs 7(b)(i) and (ii), Company shall refer to accounting statements rendered to Artist through the end of the accounting period following the earlier of (i) the date nine (9) months following Company's initial release of each applicable LP or (ii) the date upon which the LP for which the Advance Recording Fund is being determined is delivered. It is understood that in no event shall any**

**ANALYSIS**

opinion, too low. While this contract calls for fifty percent (50%) of the artist advance to be paid upon commencement of recording and the balance is paid upon delivery of the LP in some situations where the artist has more leverage this type of provision may be changed requiring one-half of the advance to be payable upon commencement of recording, one-quarter upon completion of basic tracks, and the balance upon delivery. Once again, note that the advances are recoupable from any monies payable under this or any other agreement. This is a very good phrase for the production company to have in the contract but a bad phrase for the artist. Wherever possible, I would recommend the production company have this type of phrase inserted in the contract because it means, if the artist signs Across the Board contracts with the production company, the production company may recoup the advances made under this contract from any royalties or earnings due the artist from the other contracts. This concept is called "Cross-Collateralization" of the agreements and can be justified by the production company because their investment in producing, manufacturing and promoting the artists recordings should entitle them to be able to recoup the advances as soon as possible from any source of revenue earned by the artist. From the artist's perspective, it is preferable to limit the recoupment of the costs of recording to royalties generated solely from the recordings and not any other revenue sources.

**CONTRACT**

**Advance exceed the applicable Maximum Advance set forth in subparagraph 7(d) hereof.**

**(d) (i) With respect to the Second LP and the Third LP, if any, the Base Advance shall be Fifteen Thousand Dollars ($15,000.00) and the Maximum Advance shall be Thirty Thousand Dollars ($30,000.00);**

**(ii) With respect to the Fourth LP and the Fifth LP, if any, the Base Advance shall be Twenty Thousand Dollars ($20,000.00) and the Maximum Advance shall be Forty Thousand Dollars ($40,000.00);**

**(iii) With respect to the Sixth LP and the Seventh LP, if any, the Base Advance shall be Twenty-Five Thousand Dollars ($25,000.00) and the Maximum Advance shall be Fifty Thousand Dollars ($50,000.00);**

**(iv) With respect to the Eighth LP, and any further LPs required to be recorded pursuant to the applicable Distribution Agreement, if any, the Base Advance shall be Thirty Thousand Dollars ($30,000.00) and the Maximum Advance shall be Sixty Five Thousand Dollars ($65,000.00);**

**(e) In the event Company shall require Artist to record and deliver masters consisting of less than an LP, the advance otherwise**

**ANALYSIS**

Therefore the artist will not want this agreement cross collateralized with the other contract. If the artist lives in, or has significant contacts with the state of California, the contract paragraph dealing with advances should also contain a provision regarding the payment of minimum per year advances, to each member of the artist, in order to make the injunctive provisions of the contract enforceable. I will discuss this issue further later on in this book.

| CONTRACT | ANALYSIS |
|---|---|
| payable for such masters shall be computed by multiplying the applicable advance for the preceding LP by a fraction, the numerator of which is the number of masters which Company requests and the denominator of which is ten (10). | |

(f) The Advances provided above shall be paid to Artist as follows:

(i) Fifty percent (50%) promptly following commencement of recording the applicable LP; and

(ii) The balance (less any previous payments made to or on behalf of Artist) following delivery of the applicable LP.

(g) All monies paid to Artist or on behalf of Artist or to or on behalf of any person, firm or corporation representing Artist, other than royalties payable pursuant to Paragraph 10 of this Agreement, shall constitute advances recoupable from any monies payable under this or any other agreement, unless Company shall otherwise consent in writing.

(h) With respect to payments to be made on delivery, Company shall have the right to withhold a reasonable portion thereof to provide for anticipated costs which have not yet been paid by Company or billed to Company which costs are otherwise de-

**CONTRACT**

ductible from payments to be made to Artist.

8. (a) Upon receipt of invoices therefor, Company agrees to pay all recording costs actually incurred in the production of the masters comprising each LP required to be delivered hereunder, provided such costs have been approved by Company in writing.

(b) All recording costs incurred in excess of the applicable approved recording budget shall be Artist's sole responsibility and Artist hereby agrees to forthwith pay and discharge all such excess costs. In the event Company agrees to pay any such excess costs on Artist's behalf, Artist shall, upon demand, reimburse Company for such excess costs or in lieu of requesting reimbursement, Company may deduct such excess costs from any monies due Artist under this or any other agreement. All recording costs paid by Company shall be advances against and recoupable by Company out of all royalties becoming payable to Artist pursuant to this or any other agreement.

(c) It is of the essence of this Agreement that Artist obtain prior to each applicable recording session and deliver to Company within forty-eight (48) hours following each such recording session, a duly completed and executed Form I-9 (or such similar or other form(s) as

**ANALYSIS**

**CONTRACT** | **ANALYSIS**

may be prescribed by the United States Immigration and Naturalization Service or other government agency regarding citizenship, permanent residency or so-called "documented worker" status) in respect of each individual employed to render services in the recording of masters hereunder. Artist shall simultaneously obtain and deliver to Company true and complete copies of all evidentiary documents relating to the contents or subject matter of said form(s). In the event Artist fails to comply with any of the foregoing requirements, Company may deduct any resulting penalty payments from any and all monies due under this or any other agreement.

(d) Nothing in this Agreement shall obligate Company to continue or permit the continuation of any recording session(s), even if previously approved hereunder, if Company reasonably anticipates that the recording costs for the applicable masters will exceed the amount authorized by Company or that said masters will not be commercially satisfactory.

9. (a) Each master subject hereto shall be produced by a producer approved by Company. Company hereby approves [Producer's Name] as the producer of masters subject hereto. Company shall be solely responsible for and shall pay all monies becoming payable to such producer.

## CONTRACT

**10. Conditioned upon Artist's full and faithful performance of each and all of the terms hereof, Company shall pay Artist the following royalties in respect of records subject to this Agreement:**

**(a) (i) (A) A royalty of six percent (6%) in respect of retail sales in the United States of Singles and Maxi-singles derived from masters recorded and delivered during the Term;**

**(B) The royalty rate hereinabove set forth in subparagraph 10(a)(1)(A) shall be hereinafter referred to as the "Basic U.S. Singles Rate".**

**(ii) (A) A royalty of eight percent (8%) in respect of retail sales in the United States of LPs derived from masters recorded and delivered during the Term;**

**(B) The royalty rate hereinabove set forth in subparagraph 10(a)(ii)(A) shall be hereinafter referred to as the "Basic U.S. LP Rate".**

**(C) In the event any LP which solely embodies Artist's newly recorded studio performances required to be recorded and delivered hereunder shall have net sales, full priced as initially released, through normal retailer channels in the United States in excess of 500,000 but less than 1,000,001, royalty-bearing copies,**

## ANALYSIS

10. Most new artists can expect a royalty rate in the range of 4%–10% of the retail selling price of an LP depending on a number of factors. If the record company computes its royalties on a wholesale basis the royalty rate will be double the retail royalty rate. One of the factors to be considered in determining the royalty may be whether or not the artist also produces its own recordings. If so, the artist should receive a royalty on the higher side of the spectrum. If an artist can self produce an entire LP, the royalty could approach 12%. Some superstar artist/producer may receive royalties as high as 18%–20%. In today's market, a new artist royalty rate of 6–8% of the retail selling price is reasonable. In this illustration I am assuming that the production company receives a royalty of 12% from the distributor. Under this provision the production company is required to pay the artist, who is not self producing a royalty of 8%. The difference, 4%, between the 8% royalty paid to the artist and the 12% royalty received by the production company may be the royalty used to compensate the producers of the artist's LP. Since producer's royalties usually range from 2–3% of retail, the production company is allowed to retain a 1–2% royalty for itself. This paragraph also contains an escalation provision giving the production company an additional .5% for sales in excess of 500,000 up to 1,000,000 units. These royalty rates are applicable for USA sales only.

**CONTRACT** | **ANALYSIS**

Company shall pay Artist an additional royalty of one-half percent (1/2%), but only with respect to those net sales, full priced as initially released, through normal retailer channels in the United States, in excess of 500,000, but less than 1,000,001 royalty-bearing copies of that particular LP;

(D) In the event such LP shall have further net sales, full priced as initially released, through normal retailer channels in the United States in excess of 1,000,000 royalty-bearing copies, Company shall pay Artist a further additional royalty of one-half percent (1/2%), but only with respect to those net sales, full priced as initially released, through normal retailer channels in the United States, in excess of 1,000,000 royalty-bearing copies of that particular LP.

(iii) (A) With respect to EPs, the royalty rate shall be three-fourths (3/4) of the applicable Basic U.S. LP Rate.

(B) The royalty rate hereinabove set forth in subparagraph 10(a)(iii)(A) shall be hereinafter referred to as the "Basic U.S. EP Rate".

(b) (i) (A) With respect to retail sales of Singles and Maxi-singles in Canada and the United Kingdom, the royalty rate shall be two-thirds (2/3) of the Basic U.S. Singles Rate.

**CONTRACT**

(B) With respect to retail sales of Singles and Maxi-singles outside the United States and outside those territories referred to in subparagraph 10(b)(i)(A) above, the royalty rate shall be one-half (1/2) of the Basic U.S. Singles Rate.

(C) The royalty rates hereinabove set forth in subparagraphs 10(b)(i)(A) and (B) shall each be hereinafter referred to as a "Basic Foreign Singles Rate".

(ii) (A) With respect to retail sales of LPs in Canada and the United Kingdom, the royalty rate shall be two-thirds (2/3) of the applicable Basic U.S. LP Rate.

(B) With respect to retail sales of LPs outside the United States and outside those territories referred to in subparagraph 10(b)(ii)(A) above, the royalty rate shall be one-half (1/2) of the applicable Basic U.S. LP Rate.

(C) The royalty rates hereinabove set forth in subparagraphs 10(b)(ii)(A) and (B) shall each be hereinafter referred to as a "Basic Foreign LP Rate".

(iii) (A) With respect to retail sales of EPs outside the United States, the royalty rate shall be three-fourths (3/4) of the applicable Basic Foreign LP Rate.

**ANALYSIS**

**CONTRACT**

(B) The royalty rate hereinabove set forth in subparagraph 10(b)(iii)(A) shall be hereinafter referred to as the "Basic Foreign EP Rate".

(iv) (A) Notwithstanding anything to the contrary contained herein, with respect to records sold in Brazil, Greece, Portugal, India, Kenya, Zambia, Zimbabwe, Nigeria and any other territory in which governmental or other authorities place limits on the royalty rates permissible for remittances to the United States in respect of records sold in such territory(ies), the royalty rate payable to Artist hereunder in respect of sales of records in such territory(ies) shall equal the lesser of (1) the applicable Basic Foreign Singles Rate, applicable Basic Foreign EP Rate or applicable Basic Foreign LP Rate, as the case may be or (2) the effective royalty rate permitted by such governmental or other authority for remittances to the United States less a royalty equivalent to three percent (3%) of the retail list price and such monies as Company or its licensees shall be required to pay to all applicable union funds in respect of said sales.

(B) Royalties in respect of sales of records outside the United States shall be computed in the same national currency as Company is accounted to by its licensees and shall be paid to Artist at the same rate of exchange as

**ANALYSIS**

In most recording agreements, reduced royalties are paid for non-conventional and non-USA retail sales. Sales to the government (military bases), record clubs, foreign countries etc., are reduced (at rates of sometimes one-half of the basic U.S.

**CONTRACT**

**Company is paid. It is understood that such royalties will not be due and payable until payment thereof is received by Company in the United States of America. In the event Company is unable to receive payment in United States dollars in the United States due to governmental regulations, royalties therefor shall not be credited to Artist's account during the continuance of such inability except that (1) if any accounting rendered to Artist hereunder during the continuance of such inability shows Artist's account to be in a credit position, Company will, after Artist's request and at Artist's expense, if Company is able to do so, deposit such royalties to Artist's credit in the applicable foreign currency in a foreign depository, or (2) if the royalties not credited to Artist's account exceed the amount, if any, by which Artist's account is in a debit position, then Company will, after Artist's request and at Artist's expense, and if Company is able to do so, deposit such excess royalties to Artist's credit in the applicable foreign currency in a foreign depository. Deposit as aforesaid shall fulfill Company's obligations under this Agreement as to record sales to which such royalty payments are applicable.**

**(c) With respect to records sold (i) through any direct mail or mail order distribution method, including, without limitation, record club**

**ANALYSIS**

royalty rates). Considering the fact that R&B artists sell particularly well at military bases, a request for a royalty of seventy five percent (75%) instead of fifty percent (50%) of the U.S. base royalty rate is not entirely out of line for these types of sales. Some companies may agree with the request, others won't.

Record clubs, where in some cases up to ten (10) free CDs are given to new customers, are also a sore spot for many artists. Usually the artist is only

**CONTRACT**

distribution, whether or not such record club is affiliated with Company, (ii) by distribution through retail outlets in conjunction with special advertisements on radio or television, or (iii) by any combination of the methods set forth above, the royalty payable in connection therewith shall be one-half (1/2) of Company's net earned royalty receipts in respect of reported sales through such channels. No royalties shall be payable with respect to records given away as "bonus" or "free" records as a result of joining a record club or plan or of purchasing a required number of records or with respect to records received by members of any such club operation either in an introductory offer in connection with joining such club or upon recommending that another join such club operation, provided, however, that for the purposes hereof, the number of non-royalty bearing club records shall not exceed fifty percent (50%) of the total number of records distributed through such means.

(d) With respect to mid-priced records, the royalty rate shall be two-thirds (2/3) of the applicable royalty rate payable in respect of full-priced records in the same configuration or format.

(e) With respect to budget records, the royalty rate shall be one-half (1/2) of the applicable royalty rate payable in respect of full-priced records in the same configu-

**ANALYSIS**

paid fifty percent (50%) of the U.S. royalty base rate for these sales and are not paid at all for the LPs given free to new members of the club. As a result, some hit artists have had their contracts re-negotiated to eliminate the sale of their LPs through record clubs.

**CONTRACT**

ration or format. During the Term, Company shall not release in the United States any such budget LP comprised solely of masters delivered hereunder prior to eighteen (18) months following Company's initial United States release of a full-priced record embodying such masters, unless Artist shall consent thereto.

(f) Notwithstanding anything to the contrary contained in this Agreement, in the event that Company (or its licensee(s)) shall in any country(ies) of the Territory adopt a policy applicable to the majority of LPs in Company's (or its licensee(s)') then current catalogue pursuant to which the retail list price of an LP is reduced subsequent to its initial release, then the royalty rates otherwise payable to Artist under this Agreement shall be reduced in the proportion that such reduced retail list price of the applicable LP bears to the retail list price of such LP as initially released in the applicable country.

(g) Notwithstanding anything contained herein, with respect to records in compact-disc form and records in digital audio tape form ("DAT"), the royalty rate payable shall be seventy-five percent (75%) of the Basic U.S. Singles Rate, Basic U.S. LP Rate, Basic U.S. EP Rate, applicable Basic Foreign Singles Rate, applicable Basic Foreign LP Rate or applicable Basic Foreign EP Rate, as the case may be.

**ANALYSIS**

**CONTRACT**

(h) In the event that Company shall sell or license third parties to sell "records" via telephone, satellite, cable or other direct transmission to the consumer over wire or through the air ("Satellite Sales"), Artist shall be paid royalties with respect thereto at the Basic U.S. Singles Rate, Basic U.S. LP Rate, applicable Basic U.S. EP Rate, applicable Basic Foreign Singles Rate, applicable Basic Foreign LP Rate or applicable Basic Foreign EP Rate, as the case may be. For purposes of calculating royalties payable in connection with such sales, the retail list price of such "records" shall be deemed to be the then-current retail list price of tape copies of such records and in the case records which have no tape equivalent, the corresponding price of the disc (but in the United States, eighty-five percent (85%) of the then-current retail list price of such tape copies or corresponding disc).

(i) The royalty rate payable for records sold to the United States government, its subdivisions, departments and agencies, and to educational institutions and libraries shall be one-half (1/2) of the otherwise applicable basic U.S. rate and shall be based upon the retail list price (Post Exchange list price where applicable) of such records.

(j) The royalty rate payable for records sold as "premiums" shall be one-half (1/2) of the otherwise applicable royalty rate, and the retail

**ANALYSIS**

**CONTRACT**

list price for such records shall be deemed to be Company's actual sales price. It is understood that Company shall not use Artist's name or likeness in connection with any such "premium" record as an endorsement of any product or service.

(k) Company shall have the right to license the masters to third parties for record use and/or all other types of use on a flat-fee basis. Company shall credit Artist's royalty account with fifty percent (50%) of the net amount received by Company under each such license after Company shall have first deducted all third party payments for which company is responsible.

(l) As to records not consisting entirely of masters recorded and delivered hereunder, the royalty rate otherwise payable to Artist hereunder with respect to sales of any such record shall be prorated by multiplying such royalty rate by a fraction, the numerator of which is the number of masters recorded and delivered hereunder embodied on such record and the denominator of which is the total number of masters embodied thereon.

(m) As to masters embodying performances of Artist together with the performances of another artist or artists, the royalty rate otherwise payable hereunder

**ANALYSIS**

| CONTRACT | ANALYSIS |
| --- | --- |
| with respect to sales of any record derived from any such master and the recording costs and/or advances otherwise payable by Company hereunder with respect to any such master shall be prorated by multiplying such royalty rate or recording costs and/or advances by a fraction, the numerator of which is one and the denominator of which is the total number of artists whose performances are embodied on such Master. | |
| (n) Company shall have the right to include or to license others to include any one or more of the masters in promotional records on which such masters and other recordings are included, which promotional records are designed for sale at a substantially lower price than the regular price of Company's LPs. No royalties shall be payable on sales of such promotional records. | |
| (o) No royalties shall be payable in respect of: (i) records given away or furnished on a "no-charge" basis to "one-stops", rack jobbers, distributors or dealers, whether or not affiliated with Company, which records do not exceed 300 non-royalty bearing Singles out of every 1,000 Singles distributed and 200 non-royalty bearing LPs out of every 1,000 LPs distributed; (ii) such additional "no-charge" records distributed during short term special promotions or marketing campaigns, which such | Because no royalties are paid to the artist for bonus and/or free goods, sometimes limits (30% for Singles and 20% for LPs) are put on the amount of free goods a company may distribute. |

**CONTRACT**

records do not exceed the limits set forth in subparagraph 10(o)(i) above plus an additional ten percent (10%) of the total number of records distributed; (iii) records given away or sold at below stated wholesale prices for promotional purposes to disc jockeys, record reviewers, radio and television stations and networks, motion picture companies, music publishers, Company's employees, Productions, Artist or other customary recipients of promotional records or for use on transportation facilities; (iv) records sold as scrap, salvage, overstock or "cut-outs"; (v) records sold below cost; (vi) "sampler" records intended for free distribution to automobile purchasers and containing not more than two (2) masters delivered hereunder. No royalties shall be payable on any sales by Company's licensees until payment has been received by Company in the United States.

(p) As to records sold at a discount to "one-stops", rack jobbers, distributors or dealers, whether or not affiliated with Company, in lieu of the records given away or furnished on a "no-charge" basis as provided in subparagraphs 10(o)(i) and (ii) above, the applicable royalty rate otherwise payable hereunder with respect to such records shall be reduced in the proportion that said discount wholesale price bears to the usual stated wholesale price, provided that said

**ANALYSIS**

| CONTRACT | ANALYSIS |
| --- | --- |
| **reduction in the applicable royalty rate does not exceed the percentage limitations set forth in subparagraphs 10(o)(i) and (ii) above.** | |
| **(q) The royalty rates provided for in this Paragraph 10 shall be applied against the retail list price (less Company's container deductions, excise taxes, duties and other applicable taxes) for ninety percent (90%) of records sold which are paid for and not returned. The term "retail list price" as used in this Agreement shall mean (i) for records sold in the United States, the manufacturer's suggested retail price in the United States and (ii) for records sold outside the United States, the manufacturer's suggested retail price in the country of manufacture or sale, as Company is paid. In those countries where a manufacturer's suggested retail price is not utilized, the generally accepted retail price shall be utilized. Notwithstanding the foregoing, the retail list price for a "Maxi-single" shall be deemed to be the retail list price for a Single. In computing sales, Company shall have the right to deduct all returns made at any time and for any reason.** | The royalty rates are applied against the retail list price less container deductions and excise taxes, for 90% of records sold. Why not 100% instead of 90% of records sold? The 10% is considered a "breakage deduction." This provision is a vestige of recording contracts from the 1950s when records (45s, 78s, and LPs), were made of vinyl and the record company could count on at least 10% of the records breaking during the distribution process. I wish I could say this provision is outdated but I can't. Even though the chance of CDs and cassettes breaking from factory to store shelves has been practically eliminated, some (not all) companies are still adamant about keeping this type of provision in their contracts. As you will notice in the accounting statement regarding record earnings, this 10% deduction "off the top" will invariably result in lower royalties to the artist. |
| **(r) Company's container deductions shall be a sum equal to: (i) twelve and one-half percent (12-1/2%) of the retail list price for records in disc form (other than compact-disc records), (ii) fifteen percent (15%) of the retail list price** | Another significant deduction from the retail selling price, prior to calculating royalties, is the "container deduction." The container deduction percentages of 20% for cassettes and 25% for CDs are usually a part of most major label recording agree- |

**CONTRACT**

**for records in disc form (other than compact-disc records) in "double-fold" jackets or covers or in jackets which contain an insert or any other special elements; (iii) twenty percent (20%) of the retail list price for records in analog pre-recorded tape form, and (iv) twenty-five percent (25%) of the retail list price for Satellite Sales, compact-disc records, records in digital pre-recorded tape form, and any other form or configuration of record or form of package, container or box other than as described herein.**

**11. The royalty rates provided in Paragraph 10 of this Agreement are inclusive of all royalties due to Artist as well as any other artists or third parties (excluding producers). In the event Company pays any royalties to such third parties directly, such sums shall be deducted from any and all monies otherwise payable to Artist hereunder.**

**12. Company will send Artist royalty accountings along with payment of royalties due, if any, ninety (90) days after each June 30th and December 31st for the preceding half yearly period or sixty (60) days following Company's receipt of accounting statements and remittances, if any, pursuant to the Distribution Agreement or a Successor Distribution Agreement,whichever is later. Company may charge Artist's account and deduct from those payments otherwise due**

**ANALYSIS**

ments. It's upsetting to know that the record company makes this deduction which amounts to $4.00 for a CD and $3.00 for a cassette when the record company's actual cost of manufacturing each unit (including the containers) may not exceed $1.00. Most companies take a hard line and refuse to budge when asked to reduce these percentages and it's a point I take exception to every time.

12. The production company is required to account to the artist semi-annually, within 90 days of June 30 and Dec. 31 of each calendar year. However, if the production company has a distribution agreement, as is the case here, the artist may be accounted to within 60 days following the production company's receipt of an accounting statement from the distributor.

**CONTRACT** | **ANALYSIS**

Artist recording costs and any payments made to Artist or on Artist's behalf after June 30th and December 31st but prior to the rendition of the applicable royalty statement. Company will retain a reserve against all payable royalties as is reasonable in Company's best business judgment, which reserve shall not exceed the maximum reserve provided for in the applicable Distribution Agreement and shall be liquidated as provided in such Distribution Agreement. For accounting purposes, sales of Records by Company's licensees (including, without limitation, Company's foreign licensee) if any, will be considered to have occurred in the semiannual accounting period in which Company received accounting statements and payment in the United States and in United States currency for such sales. If a licensee, (including, without limitation, Company's foreign subsidiaries and affiliates) deducts or withholds taxes of any kind from its royalty payments to Company or if such royalties are subject to currency conversion, bank or transfer charges, Company will deduct a pro rata share from Artist's royalties. In accounting to Artist, Company shall have the absolute right to rely upon the statements received by Company from the Distributor and Company shall not be responsible for any error, omission or other inaccuracy of any such statement. This Agreement along with all royalty agreements heretofore or here-

**CONTRACT**

**after entered into between Artist and Company and/or their respective affiliates will be considered a single accounting unit. Each payment from Company to Artist under this Agreement may be made by a single company check payable to [Group Name] sent by regular mail to Artist's address above (unless Company has received a formal notice of Artist's change of address).**

**13. Artist shall have the right at Artist's sole cost and expense to appoint a Certified Public Accountant who is not then currently engaged in an outstanding audit of Company to examine Company's books and records as same pertain to sales of records subject hereto as to which royalties are payable hereunder, for a period of two (2) years from the date a specific statement is rendered and only once with respect to any such specific statement. Artist shall notify Company of Artist's election to conduct such an audit. Any such examination shall be for a reasonable duration, shall take place at Company's offices during normal business hours on not less than thirty (30) days prior written notice and shall not occur more than once in any calendar year. No suit or other action may be commenced with respect to any accounting statement (or the period to which it relates) unless objection is made in writing to Company with respect thereto within two (2) years following the date upon which such**

**ANALYSIS**

13. Who's to say the production company is accounting to the artist truthfully? This audit provision gives the artist the right to review or audit the production company's books. But there are certain limits to that right. The artist may examine the production company's books as long as the artist serves written notice at least 30 days prior to examination and such notice is given to examine the books regarding a specific accounting statement rendered within the immediate past two years. No lawsuit can be brought regarding such a statement unless an objection is made in writing within two years following the date upon which such statement is rendered. Any lawsuit must be commenced within one year of delivery of the objection.

Over the past 10 years, record companies have attempted to insert various provisions further limiting the rights of artists to audit their books. These provisions, sometimes requiring the auditor to be a C.P.A. or lawyer who currently is not auditing the same company's books on behalf

**CONTRACT**

**statement is rendered and unless suit is commenced in a court of competent jurisdiction within one (1) year following the delivery of such objection; after such period, such suit or action will be forever barred.**

**14. (a) All musical compositions or material recorded pursuant to this Agreement which are written or composed, in whole or in part by Artist or any individual member of Artist or any producer of the masters subject hereto, or which are owned or controlled, directly or indirectly, in whole or in part, by Artist or any individual member of Artist or any producer of the masters subject hereto (herein called "Controlled Compositions") shall be and are hereby licensed to Company.**

**(i) For the United States, at a royalty per selection equal to seventy-five percent (75%) of the minimum statutory per selection rate (without regard to playing time) effective on the date of commencement of recording of the masters concerned. The aforesaid seventy-five percent (75%) per selection rate shall hereinafter sometimes be referred to as the "U.S. Per Selection Rate"; and**

**(ii) For Canada, at a royalty per selection equal to seventy-five percent (75%) of the statutory per selection rate (without regard to playing time) effective on the**

**ANALYSIS**

of another artist, may further complicate and in some cases, discourage an artist from requesting an audit. The artist's representative should attempt to reduce these limitations and extend his or her right to audit the record company's books as far back in the past as possible.

14. In order for the production company and/or record company to sell a recorded version of a composition, it must get the permission, in the form of a license, from the owner of the copyright of the composition. Usually the owner of the copyright is the publisher who obtains the rights from a songwriter or author of the composition by way of a contract or transfer of rights. The publisher's job is to exploit the composition for the songwriter for which the publisher usually receives 50% of the proceeds. In the Copyright Principles section of the book, I'll explore more fully the relationship of the publisher and the songwriter. For now let's limit the analysis to the instance where the artist is also the songwriter.

The license the production company must obtain is called a mechanical license. That license gives the production and record company the right to mechanically reproduce the composition on a record (i.e., single, LP, cassette or CD). In order to simplify obtaining such a license, the U.S. copyright tribunal has set a standard royalty for the licensing of the mechanical right called the compulsory minimum statutory mechanical royalty rate which, as of the beginning of 2000, was raised to 7.55 cents

**CONTRACT**

**date of commencement of recording of the masters concerned, or, if there is no statutory rate in Canada on such date, seventy-five percent (75%) of the per selection rate (without regard to playing time) then generally utilized by major record companies in Canada. The applicable aforesaid per selection rate shall hereinafter sometimes be referred to as the "Canadian Per Selection Rate".**

**(b) Notwithstanding the foregoing, the maximum aggregate mechanical royalty rate which Company shall be required to pay in respect of any Single, Maxi-single or LP hereunder, regardless of the total number of compositions contained therein, shall not exceed two (2) times, three (3) times, and ten (10) times the applicable U.S. Per Selection Rate or Canadian Per Selection Rate, respectively, and in respect of any EP hereunder, regardless of the total number of compositions contained therein, shall not exceed the applicable U.S. Per Selection Rate or Canadian Per Selection Rate times the total number of masters contained therein.**

**(c) It is specifically understood that in the event that any Single, Maxi-single, EP or LP contains other compositions in addition to the Controlled Compositions and the aggregate mechanical royalty rate for said Single, Maxi-single, EP or LP shall exceed the applicable rate provided in subparagraph**

**ANALYSIS**

per mechanical reproduction of a composition. This means that for each mechanical reproduction, be it a single, cassette or CD, the production company/record company must pay the copyright owner, who is usually the publisher, 7.55 cents for each composition contained on the configuration *unless agreed otherwise*.

Due to its investment in recording the artist, most production company's new artist's contracts will require that any compositions written and/or controlled by the artist, be licensed to the production company for 75% of the compulsory minimum statutory mechanical royalty rate. In other words, for a composition written entirely by the artist, the production company shall pay to the copyright owner 75% of 7.55 cents or roughly 5.66 cents per mechanical reproduction. While the 75% rate is universally objected to by most artist's attorneys, most record companies attempt to strictly adhere to a policy requiring its inclusion in most new (and some established) artists contracts.

Most production/record companies also place a limit on the total amount of mechanical royalties they have to pay for specific product configurations and require further that if the limit is exceeded the excess royalties paid will be deducted from the royalties due the artist. Many production/record companies will limit the maximum aggregate mechanical royalties they have to pay for a CD to ten times 75% of the minimum mechanical royalty rate or approximately 57¢ per CD. Suppose an artist's CD

**CONTRACT**

**14(b), the aggregate rate for the Controlled Compositions contained thereon shall be reduced by the aforesaid excess over said applicable rate. Additionally, Company shall have the right with respect to any Single, Maxi-single, EP or LP, the aggregate mechanical royalty rate for which exceeds the applicable rate provided in subparagraph 14(b) to deduct such excess payable thereon from any and all monies payable to Artist pursuant to this or any other agreement. All mechanical royalties payable hereunder shall be paid on the basis of net records sold hereunder for which royalties are payable to Artist pursuant to this Agreement. Company may maintain reserves with respect to payment of mechanical royalties. If Company makes an overpayment of mechanical royalties in respect of compositions recorded under this Agreement, Artist will reimburse Company for same, failing which Company may recoup any such overpayment from any monies becoming payable to Artist pursuant to this or any other agreement. Mechanical royalty payments on records subsequently returned are considered overpayments. Notwithstanding anything to the contrary contained herein, mechanical royalties payable in respect of Controlled Compositions for sales of records for any use other than as described in subparagraphs 10(a), (b) and (g) hereof**

**ANALYSIS**

contains 12 compositions, seven of which were composed by the artist and five of which were written by third-party songwriters who insist upon being paid 100%, instead of 75% of the mechanical royalty rate for their compositions. In such a case, the total mechanical royalties owed by the production/record company would be approximately 70¢ per CD or 13¢ in excess of the limit imposed by this type of provision. As a result, the artist's mechanical royalties will be reduced by such excess or 13¢ per CD. In other words, the production company and record company is getting to include some of the artist's compositions on the CD for free. My advice to artists who have these types of provisions in their contract is to allow only ten compositions on the CD if that's all you're going to be paid for and make sure all compositions written by third party songwriters are made subject to the 75% rate provisions of this contract. Companies will also attempt to limit the aggregate amount of mechanical royalties paid for singles and maxi singles to usually two or three times the 75% rate respectively. In the mid 1990's the norm was for maxi singles to contain a number of remixed versions of the same song. As a result, companies started inserting a provision in their contracts limiting the payment of mechanical royalties for the composition to one time only no matter how many versions of the composition appeared on the product. These types of provisions are still popular today and their

**CONTRACT**

**shall be seventy-five percent (75%) of the otherwise applicable U.S. Per Selection Rate or Canadian Per Selection Rate, as the case may be. Controlled Compositions which are arranged versions of any musical compositions in the public domain, when furnished by Artist for recording hereunder, shall be free of copyright royalties. Any assignment of the ownership or administration of copyright in any Controlled Composition shall be made subject to the provisions hereof and any inconsistencies between the terms of this Agreement and mechanical licenses issued to and accepted by Company shall be determined by the terms of this Agreement. If any Single, Maxi-single, EP or LP contains compositions which are not Controlled Compositions, Artist will obtain for Company's benefit mechanical licenses covering such compositions on the same terms and conditions applicable to Controlled Compositions pursuant to this Paragraph 14.**

**15. (a) In the event Company approves the production of a video, the cost of such video will be limited to specifically pre-approved sums necessary to make the applicable video and will be fully recoupable from any royalties at any time payable to Artist hereunder. Company shall credit Artist's royalty account with Fifty percent (50%) of the net receipts Company receives in connection with the commercial exploitation of such**

**ANALYSIS**

inclusion in the contract should also be resisted by the artist.

15.(a) Most mainstream artists require videos for at least two singles per LP in order to give the LP a chance of "breaking" (selling a lot of units). The costs of videos can be staggering and could range from $20,000 to $1,000,000 or more each to produce. Video costs have come to be considered an additional expense recoupable from an artist's royalties which makes it even more difficult for the artist to recoup and, therefore, be entitled to record royalties. This is

**CONTRACT**

**video. Artist acknowledges that Company is under no obligation to produce a video at any time. However, if Company does produce a video, in respect of all Controlled Compositions performed in such video, Company is hereby granted an irrevocable perpetual worldwide license to record and reproduce such Composition in such video and to distribute and perform such video and to authorize others to do so. Company will not be required to make any payment in connection with those uses of the Controlled Composition and that license will apply whether or not Company receives any payment in connection with those video(s).**

**(b) The selection to be embodied in any video and the producer, director, concept, script, production dates and locations of each such video shall be designated by Company. Company (or Distributor) shall engage the producer, director, and other production personnel for each video and Company shall be responsible and shall pay the production costs incurred in the production of each video in an amount not in excess of a budget to be established in advance by Company (the "Production Budget"). Artist shall be responsible for and shall pay all production costs for each video in excess of the Production Budget ("Excess Production Costs"). In the event Company or Distributor shall pay any such Excess Produc-**

**ANALYSIS**

because usually 50% to 100% of video costs are usually recoupable from the artist's record royalties. In this contract you will notice that 100% of the video costs are recoupable but this is an extreme position for a production/record company to take. Usually most production/ record company's contracts will provide that only 50% of the video costs may be recouped from record royalties and 100% of said costs may be recouped from royalties due the artist from receipts from commercial exploitation of the video such as in home video sales. What this contract does not provide for is a specific provision for payment of royalties for the sale of videos. While the use of the video for airing on such video outlets as MTV or BET, does not require a payment of royalties due to its promotional nature, the commercial exploitation of videos should require some form of payment. The terms of such payments vary from contract to contract. In this contract the record company is required to pay a royalty equivalent to the basic record royalty rate. A better contract may provide for the payment of a higher royalty, such as 20–30% of the gross proceeds of video sales less a distribution fee.

**CONTRACT**

tion Costs (which Company is in no way obligated to do), Artist shall promptly reimburse Company for such Excess Production Costs on demand, and, without limiting Company's other rights and remedies, Company may deduct an amount equal to such Excess Production Costs from any monies payable to Artist under this or any other agreement. Artist's compensation for performing in such videos (as opposed to Artist's compensation with respect to the commercial exploitation of such video as provided for in subparagraph 15(a) hereof) shall be limited to any minimum amounts required to be paid for such performances pursuant to any collective bargaining agreements pertaining thereto, provided, however, that Artist hereby waives any right to receive compensation to the extent such right may be waived.

(c) Company or its designee shall be the sole owner of all worldwide rights in and to each video (including, without limitation, the worldwide copyrights therein and thereto). In all other respects (e.g., the times for accountings to be rendered, and warranties and representations made by Artist) videos shall be governed by the same terms and conditions as are applicable to masters subject to this Agreement.

16. During the Term, Artist shall not perform for the purpose of

**ANALYSIS**

**CONTRACT**

making records for anyone other than Company and shall not authorize the use of Artist's name, likeness or other identification for the purpose of distributing, selling, advertising or exploiting records for anyone other than Company. Artist shall not perform any selection recorded hereunder or embodied on a master delivered hereunder for the purpose of making records for any one other than Company for distribution in the Territory (i) for a period of five (5) years after the date of delivery of the respective master containing such selection or (ii) for a period of two (2) years after the expiration or other termination of this Agreement, whichever is later ("Re-recording Restriction").

17. (a) In the event that Artist for any reason fails to timely fulfill all of Artist's producing and delivery commitments hereunder in accordance with all of the material terms and conditions of this Agreement, then, in addition to any other rights or remedies which Company may have, Company shall have the right, upon written notice to Artist at any time prior to the expiration of the then current Period, (i) to terminate this Agreement without further obligation to Artist, except the obligation to pay royalties, if due, or (ii) to reduce the minimum number of masters required to be recorded and delivered during the then current Period to the number which have been timely recorded

**ANALYSIS**

**CONTRACT** | **ANALYSIS**

and delivered during such Period. It is specifically understood that Company may exercise any or all of its rights pursuant to subparagraphs 17(a)(i) and (ii) at any time(s) prior to the date the Term would otherwise expire. Company's obligations hereunder shall be suspended for the duration of any such default. If Company terminates the Term hereof pursuant to subparagraph 17(a)(i) hereof, Company may require Artist to repay to Company the amount not then recouped of any advance previously paid by Company in connection with unrecorded or undelivered masters.

(b) Company reserves the right, at its election, to suspend the operation of this Agreement for the duration of any of the following contingencies, if by reason of any such contingency, it is materially hampered in the performance of its obligations under this Agreement or its normal business operations are delayed or become impossible or commercially impracticable: Act of God, fire, catastrophe, labor disagreement, acts of government, its agencies or officers, any order, regulation, ruling or action of any labor union or association of artists, musicians, composers or employees affecting Company or the industry in which it is engaged, delays in the delivery of materials and supplies, or any other cause beyond Company's control. Any such suspension due to a labor controversy

**CONTRACT**

**which involves only Company shall be limited to a period of six (6) months.**

**(c) Artist acknowledges that Artist's services hereunder are special, unique as intellectual character which gives them peculiar values and in the event of a breach or threatened breach by Artist of any term, condition or covenant hereof, Company will be caused irreparable injury and Company shall be entitled to injunctive and other equitable relief in addition to any other rights or remedies, as otherwise available to Company.**

**18. (a) Artist warrants and represents that: (i) Artist has the full right and authority to grant Company all of the rights set forth in this Agreement free and clear of any claims, rights and obligations; (ii) Artist has not granted nor will at any time grant to any third parties any rights which are inconsistent with the rights granted to Company in this Agreement; (iii) the masters and material embodied in the masters are not and will not be imitations or copies, and will not infringe upon any common law, statutory law or other rights of any person, firm or corporation; (iv) Artist's professional name will throughout the Term continue to**

**ANALYSIS**

17.(c) The insertion of this exclusivity provision includes an acknowledgement of the uniqueness and special intellectual character of the artist's services and establishes the production company's basis to prevent the artist from performing for another label after the mere allegation of a breach of the agreement. If the artist fails to perform for the production company and attempts to provide its services to another company, the production/record company may have the right to go to court to prevent the artist from doing so. Over the years, this type of provision has been the focus of a great deal of litigation and regulation and will be discussed further in Paragraph 22.

18. The production/record company requires the artist to guarantee: 1) that it has the right to enter the agreement free and clear; 2) that the artist cannot be bound to another contract which will interfere with this one; 3) the Masters will not infringe on common or statutory rights of another person; 4) the artist's professional name shall be solely owned by the company; and 5) each member of artist is of legal age. If not, the laws of the state in which the minor resides must be satisfied to bind the minor.

As indicated in an earlier section, the production/record company's ownership of the group name can be a problem to the group's use of the name should the contract be termi-

**CONTRACT**

**be the sole property of Company for all purposes and will, during the Term, be used solely by Company and its licensees in connection with exploitation of records; (v) each member comprising Artist is above the legal age of majority pursuant to the laws governing this Agreement and the performance hereunder; (vi) the materials do not now and will not at any time hereafter infringe upon any copyright, trademark, right of privacy or publicity and does not and will not at any time constitute a libel, slander or defamation of any party; and (vii) Company will not be required to make any payments in connection with the acquisition, exercise or exploitation of its rights pursuant to this Agreement except as specifically provided for in this Agreement.**

**(b) Artist indemnifies and holds Company, its assignees, etc., harmless from any damages, liabilities, costs, losses and expenses (including legal costs and reasonable attorneys' fees) arising out of or connected with any claim, demand or action by a third party which is inconsistent with any of the warranties, representations or covenants made by any or all of Artist in this Agreement. Artist agrees to reimburse Company on demand for any payment made by Company at any time with respect to any claim, demand or action to which the foregoing indemnity applies. Pending the determination of any claims raised, Company may withhold**

**ANALYSIS**

nated. Motown owned the name "The Jackson Five." When the group left to record with Epic Records, they had to use the name "The Jackson's" instead. Years later, another group "New Edition" found itself in a similar situation after terminating its agreement with a production company owned by Maurice Starr. Mr. Starr filed a lawsuit to enjoin the group from using the name to promote a record for its new company, MCA In that case, the court found that, as a result of the name being identified with the individual group members who collectively made it popular, the group members did acquire certain property rights in the name and could not be prevented from using it.

Record/production companies also have a justifiable interest in guaranteeing that their artists aren't minors at the time of signing the record contract. Binding minors to record contracts is illegal in most states, unless there are specific regulations allowing for such. Therefore, it is important to determine if you can bind a minor to such a contract before investing money in creating the minor's first hit record. This way you don't have to worry about the minor later disaffirming the contract, leaving you high and dry. The best example of this is again provided by the New Edition/Maurice Starr relationship. Mr. Starr contracted with minors, Ricky Bell, Ronnie Devoe, Bobby Brown, Michael Bivens and Ralph Tresvant p/k/a New Edition in the state of Massachusetts, where at that

**CONTRACT**

**payment of all monies due under this Agreement in an amount consistent with such claim, demand or action.**

**19. Artist and Company each have the status of independent contractors under this Agreement and nothing in this Agreement constitutes a partnership or joint venture, nor are any or all of Artist agents or employees of Company. No other party is intended to be or will be a third party beneficiary of this Agreement.**

**20. If any provision of this Agreement is held void, invalid, illegal or inoperative, no other provision of this Agreement will be affected as a result, and, accordingly, the remaining provisions will remain in full force and effect as though the void, invalid, illegal or inoperative provision had not been contained herein.**

**21. Company will have Thirty (30) days from receipt of notice within to cure any breach of this Agreement. Artist will have a similar period, except with regard to a breach of their covenant of exclusivity or their obligations to record under this Agreement, for each of which Company may immediately obtain injunctive relief since Artist acknowledges that the individual and collective services and each of the Masters are of a special, unique and intellectual character, the loss of which would cause Company irreparable injury. Notices to either**

**ANALYSIS**

time, binding minors to personal service contracts was deemed against public policy and therefore illegal. After releasing a successful LP which launched the group to superstar status, the group disaffirmed the contract with Mr. Starr and went on to achieve even greater fame with MCA Records. The moral of this story is "don't sign minors in states where it is illegal to do so." Mr. Starr learned his lesson well, however. He later signed a contract with New Kids On The Block in the state of New York where there is a statute making contracts with minors enforceable and binding.

21. What happens if the artist feels the production company has breached the agreement? The production company must be notified of the specific breach and will have thirty (30) days to cure. This particular contract allows the artist thirty (30) days to cure a breach unless it is a breach of the artist's covenant of exclusivity in which case, under the terms of this contract, the production company may be entitled to immediate injunctive relief.

**CONTRACT**

**party will be sent to the applicable address on Page 1 of this Agreement (unless formal notice of a new address has been received), postage prepaid, by registered or certified mail and return receipt requested. Further, a copy of notices to Company will be sent to [Production Company's Attorney's Address].**

**22. Company will have no liability for any failure to request or permit completion of Artist's recording commitment hereunder unless Artist at all times is ready, willing and able to perform as and when provided herein and Company refuses to permit same. If Artist does not timely notify Company of any failure by Company to fulfill the minimum recording obligation for any Term hereof, then Company will have no liability whatsoever for or in connection with any recordings not recorded by Artist during such Term. If Artist does timely notify Company of such failure, then Company's sole obligation to Artist as to each unrecorded required master shall be to pay each Key Member of Artist the difference between any monies paid to each Key Member of Artist in connection with said Artist's recording services during the then current sequential year of the Term hereof and each Key Member of Artist will receive compensation (as defined below) of not less than the following amounts:**

**First Contract Year: Nine Thousand Dollars ($9,000.00);**

**ANALYSIS**

22. This paragraph addresses the issue of the production company obtaining an injunction. As you can see, it says that the production company's sole obligation to the artist, should production company fail to record the minimum commitment, is to pay the difference between any monies paid the artist for services during the year and the amounts set forth in this clause, referred to as the Jump Ship Clause.

### "Jump Ship" Clause "$9,000 Plus" Provision

This clause, required to be contained in California contracts, updates an earlier law enacted in 1919 which required guaranteed payments of $6,000.00 per year for a company to enjoin an "exclusive" artist from providing his/her services to another company. The newer law, as codified in Section 3423 of the California Civil Code on January 1, 1994, establishes a two tiered system requiring minimum payments for years one through three and additional compensation over and above the minimum in years four through seven ("Plus Money").

**California's Jump Ship Clause**

| *Year* | *Minimum* | *Plus* |
|---|---|---|
| 1 | $ 9,000 | -0- |
| 2 | $12,000 | -0- |
| 3 | $15,000 | -0- |
| 4 | $15,000 | $15,000 |
| 5 | $15,000 | $15,000 |
| 6 | $15,000 | $30,000 |
| 7 | $15,000 | $30,000 |

**CONTRACT**

**Second Contract Year: Twelve Thousand Dollars ($12,000.00);**

**Third Contract Year: Fifteen Thousand Dollars ($15,000.00);**

**Fourth Contract Year: Fifteen Thousand Dollars ($15,000.00);**

**Fifth Contract Year: Fifteen Thousand Dollars ($15,000.00);**

**Sixth Contract Year: Fifteen Thousand Dollars ($15,000.00);**

**Seventh (and any applicable succeeding) Contract Year: Fifteen Thousand Dollars ($15,000.00).**

**ANALYSIS**

The minimum must be paid before the end of each contract year. The Plus money must be paid at anytime prior to seeking injunction.

The statute also provides an escape hatch for companies that either fail to include a minimum compensation clause in their contract or, having included the provision, fail to fulfill their obligations thereunder referred to as the "Superstar Insurance" clause.

**Superstar Insurance Clause**

| *Contract Year* | *Ten Fold Lump Sum* | *Prior Year's Aggregate* | | *Total to be Paid for Injunction* |
|---|---|---|---|---|
| 1 | $ 90,000 | Plus -0- | = | $90,000.00 |
| 2 | $120,000 | Plus $90,000 | = | $210,000.00 |
| 3 | $150,000 | Plus $210,000 | = | $ 360,000.00 |
| 4 | $300,000 | Plus $360,000 | = | $ 660,000.00 |
| 5 | $300,000 | Plus $660,000 | = | $ 960,000.00 |
| 6 | $450,000 | Plus $960,000 | = | $ 1,410,000.00 |
| 7 | $450,000 | Plus $1,410,000 | = | $ 1,860,000.00 |

## CONTRACT

**Compensation paid in any Contract Year in excess of the minimums specified above shall apply to reduce the Compensation otherwise required above to be paid in any subsequent Contract Year. In the event the Compensation paid to any Key Member of Artist is below the amount described above as of thirty (30) days prior to the end of the applicable Contract Year, such member of Artist will give Company written notice containing specific reference to this paragraph 22(a) and specifying such deficiency. Such notice may be given no earlier than thirty (30) days not later than fifteen (15) days prior to the expiration of the Contract Year concerned. Promptly after its receipt of such notice, during the term of this agreement, Company will pay the actual amount of any such deficiency, which payment shall be a pre-payment of any monies due Artist hereunder. Any failure by Company to make such payment will not constitute a material breach of this agreement. As used in this paragraph 22(a), (1) Contract Year means the actual period beginning on the first day of the term of this agreement, as applicable, and each subsequent annual period during the continuance of the term; and (2) Compensation means all monies paid to the member of Artist (including, but not limited to, Advances and Record royalties, but not including Mechanical Royalties; and (3) Key member means (name of Member(s)) and any**

## ANALYSIS

In response, many record companies use their New York office address and have the artists agree to the use of New York law in interpreting their contracts. It is, as of yet, undetermined whether this strategy will work, particularly in a case where the artist subsequently becomes a California resident and, as such may attempt to invoke the jurisdiction of the California court system.

Some record companies may seek to blunt the effect of the law by agreeing to make the $9,000.00 plus provision applicable to only the key members of the group with the anticipated result being that the other group members will be forced to follow the lead of the Key member. Because the statute requires the minimum compensation to be stated in the contract, it is advisable to amend the agreement of any artist who may at some point, reside in California, so as to make it compatible with California law.

| CONTRACT | ANALYSIS |
|---|---|
| other member of Artist who is (a) a lead vocalist on Artist's most recent Album of the Recording Commitment, (b) a lead instrumentalist for a substantial portion of the material on Artist's most recent Album of the Recording Commitment, or (c) a producer of a substantial portion of the material on Artist's most recent Album of the Recording Commitment. | |
| Such sums paid to Artist will constitute an advance against any other monies at any time payable hereunder. Under no circumstances, however, will Company be deemed to have waived its right to any recordings which Artist is obligated to deliver hereunder unless such waiver is expressly set forth in a written instrument of waiver signed by One (1) duly authorized officer of Company. | |
| 23. Company will be the copyright proprietor of all record cover artwork and will have the unrestricted and unlimited right to utilize all artwork elements in connection with the rights granted herein, including but not limited to the manufacture, sale, advertisements and promotion of records embodying the masters and all merchandize of any kind. | |
| 24. Wherever in this Agreement Artist's approval or consent is required, such approval or consent shall not be unreasonably withheld. Company may require Artist | |

| CONTRACT | ANALYSIS |
|---|---|
| to formally give or withhold such approval or consent by giving Artist written notice requesting same and by furnishing Artist with the information or material in respect of which such approval or consent is sought. Artist shall give Company written notice of approval or disapproval within five (5) days after such notice. Artist shall not hinder nor delay the scheduled release of any record hereunder. In the event of disapproval or no consent, the reasons therefor shall be stated. Failure to give such notice to Company as aforesaid shall be deemed to be consent or approval. | |
| 25. During the Term, Artist shall become and remain a member in good standing of any labor unions with which Company may at any time have agreements lawfully requiring such union membership, including, but not limited to, the American Federation of Musicians and the American Federation of Television and Radio Artists. All masters subject hereto shall be produced in accordance with the rules and regulations of all unions having jurisdiction. | |
| 26. Company shall have the right to secure insurance with respect to Artist for Company's own benefit. In this connection, each member of Artist agrees to be available for physical examinations by a physician as and when reasonably requested to do so and to complete such questionnaires and other documents which Company or any in- | |

**CONTRACT**

**surance carrier may from time to time require in connection with securing and maintaining such insurance.**

**27. For the purposes of this Agreement, the following definitions shall apply. However, if the definitions containing in the Distribution Agreement are inconsistent with the definitions provided herein the definitions of the Distribution Agreement shall control in connection with those records distributed by Distributor.**

**(a) "Master"—The equivalent of a recording of a single selection or medley of not less than 3-1/2 minutes of playing time intended for use in the manufacture and sale of records.**

**(b) "Single"—A record embodying thereon two (2) masters.**

**(c) "Maxi-single"—A record embodying thereon not more than four (4) masters.**

**(d) "EP"—A record embodying thereon either five (5) masters or six (6) masters, provided, however, that in the event that more than one (1) of such masters embody the same musical composition, such record shall be deemed to be a Maxi-single for the purposes of this Agreement.**

**(e) "LP"—A record of not less than 35 minutes of playing**

**ANALYSIS**

27. The definitions provision of a recording contract is one of its most important components. Items that may be considered given in earlier provisions of the contract can effectively be taken away in the definitions provision.

For instance, take the definition of "Records." Throughout this Agreement the artist might have thought this contract was solely for audio cassettes/CDs and promotional videos. But when you look closely, you'll find this contract covers the artist recording for any medium, including sound synchronization with visual images. Does the artist then have the right to make its own video products which do not involve their own music such as an exercise video? Perhaps not. In Sub-Paragraph (n), "or any other agreement" is defined as: any other agreement between artist and company. Once again, cross collateralization raises its ugly head. What about advances the production/company publishing/management company makes to the artist for loans to cover expenses such as costuming, travel, band salaries for club dates? Are they recoupable under the recording agreement? Possibly, but only if a provision allowing it is inserted in the Agreement.

**CONTRACT**

time. Multiple sets which consist of more than one (1) LP intended to be released, packaged and sold together for a single overall price shall be deemed to be the equivalent of one (1) LP for the purposes of this Agreement, but shall not be recorded hereunder without Company's prior written consent.

(f) "Records", "phonograph records", "recordings" and "sound recordings"—All forms of recording and reproduction by which sound may be recorded now known or which may hereafter become known, manufactured or sold primarily for home use, juke box use, or use on or in means of transportation, including, without limiting the foregoing, magnetic recording tape, film, electronic video recordings and any other medium or device for the production of artistic performances manufactured or sold primarily for home use, juke box use or use on or in means of transportation, whether embodying (i) sound alone or (ii) sound synchronized with visual images, e.g. "sight and sound" devices.

(g) "Delivery", "deliver" or "delivered"—The actual receipt by Company of completed, fully edited, mixed, leadered and equalized masters comprising the applicable minimum recording commitment, commercially satisfactory in Company's opinion and

**ANALYSIS**

| CONTRACT | ANALYSIS |
| --- | --- |
| ready for Company's manufacture of records, together with all materials, consents, approvals, licenses and permissions.<br><br>(h) "Recording Costs"—Wages, fees, advances and payments of any nature to or in respect of all musicians, vocalists, conductors, arrangers, orchestrators, engineers, producers, copyists, etc.; payments to a trustee or fund based on wages to the extent required by any agreement between Company and any labor organization or trustee; all studio, tape, editing, mixing, re-mixing, mastering and engineering costs; all costs of travel, per diems, rehearsal halls, non-studio facilities and equipment, dub-down, rental and transportation of instruments; all costs occasioned by the cancellation of any scheduled recording session; and all other costs and expenses incurred in producing the master recordings hereunder which are then customarily recognized as recording costs in the recording industry.<br><br>(i) "mid-priced record"—A record which bears a suggested retail list price in the applicable country of the Territory of at least Two Dollars ($2.00) but not more than Three Dollars ($3.00) (or the equivalent in the applicable foreign currency) less than the suggested retail list price of Company's or Company's licensee's, as applicable, then-current newly-released | |

| **CONTRACT** | **ANALYSIS** |
|---|---|

top-line records in the same configuration or format.

(j) "budget record"—A record which bears a suggested retail list price in the applicable country of the Territory which is more than Three Dollars ($3.00) (or the equivalent in the applicable foreign currency) less than the suggested retail list price of Company's or Company's licensee's, as applicable, then-current newly released top-line records in the same configuration or format.

(k) "videos"—motion pictures and other audiovisual works that have a soundtrack substantially featuring performances of Artist.

(l) "Term"—collectively refers to the first Contract Period and all exercised Option Periods of this Agreement, however, in no event will the Term expire less than six (6) months after Artist's complete delivery of the Masters to be delivered during the last Contract Period hereof.

(m) "Territory"—the entire Universe.

(n) "or any other agreement"—Any other agreement between Artist (or any entity furnishing the services or recordings of Artist) and Company relating to the services or recordings of Artist.

(o) "Distributor"—a record

**CONTRACT** | **ANALYSIS**

company, a licensee of Company, or other entity including, without limitation MCA, WEA, CEMA, BMG Distribution, Sony Music, Inc. and Polygram, which has entered into a Distribution Agreement with Company to distribute records derived from masters hereunder. As of the date hereof, the Distributor is [Distributor's Name].

(p) "Distribution Agreement"—an Agreement between Company and a Distributor for the distribution of records embodying masters hereunder.

28. Company or its assignees will have the right to assign this Agreement and all or a portion of its rights under this Agreement.

29. This Agreement sets forth the entire agreement between any or all of Artist and Company with respect to the subject matter of this Agreement, any and all prior or contemporaneous negotiations, understandings, agreements, representations, warranties, inducements or the like heretofore made being superseded by and merged into this memorandum of agreement. No modification, amendment, waiver, termination or discharge of this memorandum of agreement or of any provision hereof shall be binding upon any party hereto unless confirmed by a written instrument signed by such party or its authorized representa-

| **CONTRACT** | **ANALYSIS** |
|---|---|
| tive. No waiver of any provision of this memorandum of agreement or of any default hereunder will affect any party's rights thereafter to enforce such provision or to exercise any right or remedy in the event of any other default, whether or not similar.<br><br>30. This Agreement shall be deemed to have been made in the State of New York and its validity, construction, performance and breach shall be governed by the laws of the State of New York applicable to agreements made and to be wholly performed therein. Artist agrees to submit to the jurisdiction of the Federal or State courts located in New York City in any action which may arise out of this Agreement and said courts shall have exclusive jurisdiction over all disputes between Company and Artist pertaining to this Agreement and all matters related thereto. In this regard, any process in any action or proceeding commenced in the courts of the State of New York arising out of any claim, dispute or disagreement under this Agreement may, among other methods, be served upon Artist by delivering or mailing the same, via registered or certified mail, addressed to Artist at the address provided herein for notices to Artist; any such delivery or mail service shall be deemed to have the same force and effect as personal service within the State of New York. Nothing contained herein shall | |

**CONTRACT**

constitute a waiver of any other remedies available to Company. Nothing contained in this Paragraph 30 shall preclude Company from joining Artist in an action brought by a third party against Company in any jurisdiction, although Company's failure to join Artist in any such action in one instance shall not constitute a waiver of any of Company's rights with respect thereto, or with respect to any subsequent action brought by a third party against Company.

31. This Agreement shall not become effective until it is executed by all parties.

32. (a) Artist warrants, represents and agrees that, for so long as this Agreement shall be in effect, they will perform together as a group (the "Group") for Company. If any individual comprising Artist refuses, neglects or fails to perform together with the other individuals comprising Artist in fulfillment of the obligations agreed to be performed under this Agreement or leaves the Group, Artist shall give Company prompt written notice thereof. Said individual shall remain bound by this Agreement, including, but not limited to, the provisions of subparagraph 32(b) hereof or Company may, by notice in writing, (i) terminate this Agreement with respect to such individual or (ii) terminate this Agreement in its entirely without any obliga-

**ANALYSIS**

32.(a) If the artist is a group, the production company will want to have a provision dealing with the potential of a member of the group either striking out on his own for a solo career or starting a new group. These "Leaving Member" provisions, as they are called, are drafted in a manner discouraging the members from leaving. It also affirms the production company's right to exclusively record the "leaving" member. Therefore, if a member, refuses, neglects or fails to perform with the group, the "Artist" must promptly notify the production company in writing triggering the production company's rights either to terminate the contract as to the disgruntled member or the group whom he or she is leaving. Also, in this case, where the production company owns the group name, the leaving member

**CONTRACT**

**tion as to unrecorded or undelivered masters. The individual whose engagement is so terminated or who refuses, neglects or fails to perform with the Group or who leaves the Group may not perform for others for the purpose of recording any selection as to which the applicable restrictive period specified in Paragraph 16 of this Agreement has not expired. Any member of the Group who refuses, neglects or fails to perform with the Group or who leaves the Group shall not thereafter use the professional name of the Group in any commercial or artistic endeavor; said professional name shall remain the property of Company. The person, if any, engaged to replace the individual whose engagement is terminated shall be approved by Company. if Company does not so approve any individual, Company may terminate this Agreement by notice in writing. In the event that an individual's engagement is terminated by notice from Company, or by mutual consent, (i) each party shall be relieved and discharged from liability for masters unrecorded at the time of such notice or mutual consent and (ii) Artist will be solely responsible for and shall pay all monies required to be paid to any individual whose engagement is so terminated in connection with all masters theretofore or thereafter recorded under this Agreement and Artist will hold Company harmless with respect thereto. Each person added to**

**ANALYSIS**

may not have the right to use the name upon leaving. If a replacement member is found, the new member must be approved by the production company and shall be required to become a party to the recording contract with the production company.

**CONTRACT** | **ANALYSIS**

Artist, as a replacement or otherwise, shall become a party to this Agreement as a condition precedent to being so added.

(b) In addition to the rights provided in the preceding subparagraph 32(a), Company shall have, and each individual comprising Artist hereby grants to Company, an irrevocable option for the individual and exclusive services of such individual(s) comprising Artist for the purpose of making records. Said option with respect to such individual(s) may be exercised by Company giving such individual(s) notice in writing within three (3) months after Company receives the notice provided for in subparagraph 32(a) to the effect that such individual(s) has refused, neglected or failed to perform with the other individuals comprising Artist or that such individual(s) has left the Group or that the Group has disbanded. In the event of Company's exercise of such option, such individual(s) shall be deemed to have entered into a new and separate agreement with Company with respect to such individual(s)' exclusive recording services upon all the terms and conditions of this Agreement except that: (i) the initial period shall be for a period of one (1) year from the date of Company's exercise of such option with an additional number of options granted to Company to extend the term of such agreement for additional consecutive one (1) year periods equal to the number of years

## CONTRACT

then remaining under this Agreement, but in no event less than three (3) additional years, which options shall be exercised by Company giving notice to such individual at any time prior to each applicable anniversary date; (ii) the minimum recording and deliver obligation shall be one (1) LP per period, provided, however, that Company shall have the right to request additional sides up to one (1) LP during each period; (iii) the provisions contained in subparagraph 10(a) of this Agreement shall not be applicable; (iv) Company shall advance all recording costs in respect of masters to be recorded by such individual up to the amount of the budget approved by Company therefor; (v) Company's royalty obligation to such individual in respect of such recordings shall be the payment to such individual of the royalties computed as set forth in this Agreement except that the Basic U.S. Singles Rate shall be five percent (5%) and the Basic U.S. LP Rate shall be seven percent (7%) with royalties for all other uses (foreign sales, clubs, licensing, etc.), reduced proportionately; (vi) Company shall be entitled to maintain a single account with respect to recordings subject to this Agreement and such agreement in respect of such individual(s); and (vii) recordings by such individual shall not be applied in diminution of Artist's minimum

## ANALYSIS

**CONTRACT**

**recording commitment as set forth in this Agreement.**

**(c) No changes in the individuals comprising Artist may be made without Company's prior written consent. Company shall have the right to change or replace members of Artist as it deems necessary in its sole judgment. Artist shall not have the right, so long as this Agreement is in effect, to assign Artist's professional name as mentioned on Page 1 hereof (or any other name(s) utilized by Artist in connection with recordings subject hereto) or to permit the use of said name(s) by any other individual or group of individuals without Company's prior written consent, and any attempt to do so shall be null and void and shall convey no right or title. The individuals comprising Artist jointly and severally represent and warrant that they are and shall be the sole owners of all such professional name(s), and that no other person, firm or corporation has the right to use said name(s) or to permit said name(s) to be used in connection with records, and that the individuals comprising Artist have the authority to grant Company the exclusive right to use said name(s) in the Territory. Company shall have the exclusive right to use said name(s) in accordance with all terms and conditions of this Agreement.**

**(d) In addition to its rights pur-**

**ANALYSIS**

32.(c) In this paragraph, you'll see an interesting statement regarding the use of the group name. You remember earlier, I mentioned that the individual group members owned no rights in the group name. Why then, in this paragraph, is reference made that the group may have ownership of the name and, if so, must give the production company the right to use the name for the purpose of selling records? Why is this provision inserted when earlier in the contract it appeared clear that the production company owned the group name? This provision was inserted in artist contracts in direct response the New Edition/Maurice Starr tradename case I mentioned earlier. In that case the court held that group members, over a course of time in which the individual members become synonymous with the group name, may accrue rights in the name, despite a production company's prior tradename registration. Therefore, this provision grants the production company the right to use the group name for purpose of selling records should the group members subsequently be ruled to have rights in the name.

**CONTRACT**

suant to subparagraphs 32 (a) and (b), Company shall have the right to record the performances of any one or more of the individuals comprising Artist without the other individuals comprising Artist upon all of the terms and conditions herein contained; provided, however, that should Company elect to do so, the provisions set forth in subparagraph 32(b) hereof shall be applied with respect to such individual or individuals whose performances are actually so recorded. In the event that any individual member of Artist wishes to record performances of any of the individual(s) comprising Artist, when such individual(s) remains a member of Artist and continues to perform their obligations hereunder, Artist shall give Company prompt notice thereof. Company shall thereafter have the irrevocable option to acquire such recordings, and if exercised, such recordings shall be acquired upon the terms set forth in subparagraph 32(b). If Company shall decline to acquire any such recordings, then Artist hereby warrants, represents and agrees that such recordings shall not be made or if made, that no use, including, but not limited to, any commercial release thereof, shall be made by Artist or anyone deriving any rights therefrom.

IN WITNESS WHEREOF, the parties hereto have executed this Agreement on the day and year first above written.

**ANALYSIS**

**CONTRACT**

AGREED TO AND ACCEPTED:
By:

______________________________

[Names of the Individual Members of Artist]

______________________________

______________________________

______________________________

IMPORTANT LEGAL DOCUMENT PLEASE CONSULT YOUR OWN ATTORNEY BEFORE SIGNING.

**ANALYSIS**

# 7

# Statement and Analysis of Recording Earnings

## *Why having a Million-Seller doesn't Mean a Million Dollar$ to the Artist.*

When I was in junior high and high school taking math and algebra classes, I would complain (along with most of my classmates!) that we would never use what we were being taught in the "real world," so what was the sense in learning it? Well, welcome to the "real world." If you want to be in this or any other business, you've got to be able to read, write, and count (as well as figure). For all of you who have talent and say you want to be in the music business, master the three R's: "Readin', 'Ritin', and 'Rithmetic," because believe me, in the real world all aspects of business are based on them.

The purpose of this analysis to show the correlation of the accounting statements to the provisions of the contracts which give rise to them. I think this is very important because it gets to the essence of the music *business*, how the money is made. Watch, as the money the production company or the artist is entitled to either flows through or is bottled up in certain provisions of the contract.

The statement of recording earnings is based on some very important assumptions. In that our sample exclusive recording artist contract is between the production company and the artist, we must first assume that another contract exists between the production company and a major distributor for the manufacture and distribution of the artist's recordings. We must also make other assumptions regarding the production company/distributor contract that will help us complete our analysis.

The first assumption is that the production company/distributor contract provides that the major distributor will pay the production company an "all-in recording fund" of $250,000 per LP and an "all-in royalty" of 12% retail. An "all-in" designation of a fund or royalty is an industry term describing how the monies for the recording will be disbursed and categorized by the distributor. In deals with new production companies most distributors will offer to pay the recording costs for the LP under what is called a "recording budget" as opposed to the preferable "all-in recording fund" method. In a recording budget type of deal, the distributor will allow the production company to spend a predetermined maximum amount for the recording of the LP, provided the costs are submitted to the distributor for direct payment on an itemized invoice basis. In this type of deal, it is necessary for the production company to account for all recording costs. If it is determined after the LP is completed that the recording costs fall short of the approved recording budget, the distributor, not the production company, keeps the balance of budget not expended. However, in an "all-in recording fund" type of agreement (as in our example), the distributor pays the production company $250,000 to record the LP. This amount is payable in its entirety directly to the production company, usually in installments of $125,000 upon commencement of recording of the LP and the balance of $125,000 upon satisfactory delivery of the LP. In exchange for the payment to the production company of the entire amount of the fund, the distributor expects, and indeed, contractually requires, the production company to pay all costs associated with the recording and delivery of the master recordings comprising the LP.

You might remember the advice I gave in the section entitled "Why Having a Million-Seller doesn't Mean a Million Dollars to the Artist?" While $250,000 sounds like a lot of money, keep in mind that there are definite costs associated with producing an LP. In the case of a production company, the key cost is recording costs, which include a wide range of expenses, such as payments to musicians, audiotape, equipment rental, recording artist advances, producer fees or advances and mastering fees, and studio costs. Sounds like a pretty daunting task, right? It is, but the beauty of the all-in-recording fund arrangement is that the production company, not the distributor, gets to keep the balance of the fund if the LP recording costs are less than the amount of the recording fund. When we do the math, we see that if the recording fund is $250,000 per LP and the production company delivers a satisfactory LP at a cost of $120,000, the production company gets to pocket $130,000.

An "all-in royalty" is similar to an "all-in-recording fund" in regard to its effect on the production company. You'll hear the term "*points*" used a lot in the record business. A point is one percentage (1%) point of either the retail price or wholesale price of either an LP or a single. In most music contracts the selling price is not the actual recommended price, but a defined term, usually less than the recommended retail or wholesale price. In an all-in-royalty type of deal, the production company receives a royalty of, as in this instance, 12%, out of which the production company must pay all royalty participants they contract with to produce or perform on the record. If the artist's royalty is six percent (6%) and the producer's royalties total three percent (3%) for the LP, the production company will be entitled to retain for itself a royalty of three percent (3%), the balance of royalties left after deduction of the artist and producer royalties.

The second assumption is that this statement covers the sale of only one (1) LP.

The third assumption is that the other provisions of the production company/distributor contract are similar to the exclusive recording artist/production company contract except that, in the production company/distributor contract, the distribution company is only allowed to recoup 50% of video and independent promotion costs from the production company's record royalties. In contrast you might remember that the production company can recoup 100% of such costs from the artist pursuant to the exclusive recording artist/production company contract.

The fourth assumption is that the LP for which the accounting statement is submitted sold 100,000 copies in the cassette configuration and 200,000 in the CD configuration. Let's first look at the advances.

| *Production Company* | | | *Contract Para. #* | *Artist* |
|---|---|---|---|---|
| | *Advances* | | | *Advances* |
| | $250,000 | From Distributor | | |
| Less | 100,000 | Recording Costs | | |
| | 20,000 | Advance to Artist | 7(a) | $20,000 From Production Co. |
| | $130,000 | Profit to Production Co. | | |

As I indicated in the first assumption, the production company received an "all-in-recording fund" of $250,000 for delivery of the LP. The recording costs are $100,000 and the artist's advance (pursuant to the exclusive recording artist/production company contract) is $20,000. Therefore, the production company keeps $130,000 of the fund. Now let's take a look at the royalties due the production company and the artist from the sale of cassettes of the LP.

## CASSETTE ROYALTIES

| *Production Company Royalties* | | | *Contract Para. #* | *Artist Royalties* |
|---|---|---|---|---|
| | $10.98 | Retail List Price | | |
| Less: | 2.20 | Packaging Deduction (20% of 10.98) | 10r(iii) | |
| | $8.78 | Royalty Base Price | | $8.78 Royalty Base Price |
| | x 12% | Production Co. Royalty Rate | | x 8% Artist Royalty Rate |
| | $1.05 | Royalty Per Cassette | | $.70 Royalty Per Cassette |

*continued*

| Production Company Royalties | | | Contract Para. # | Artist Royalties |
|---|---|---|---|---|
| | 100,000 | Cassettes Shipped | | |
| Less: | 20,000 | Free Goods (20% of 100,000) | 10o | |
| | 80,000 | Cassettes Sold | | |
| Less: | 8,000 | Breakage Deduction (10% of 80,000) | 10q | |
| | 72,000 | Royalty Bearing Cassettes | | 72,000 Royalty Bearing Cassettes |
| | x $1.05 | Royalty Per Cassette | | x $.70 Royalty per Cassette |
| | $75,600 | Cassette Royalties Due Production Co. | | $ 50,400 Cassette Royalties due Artist |

The retail list price for cassettes of most new artists' LPs is $10.98. Of course, as I indicated earlier, the *actual* retail selling price is *not* the price that the royalty percentage is applied to. As pointed out in paragraph 10r. of the exclusive recording artist/production company contract, the royalty rates are applied to the retail list price, less a container deduction, which, in the case of the cassette configuration, is 20% of the retail list price. Twenty percent (20%) of $10.98 is $2.20. That's right, $2.20. As indicated earlier, the distributor's actual cost to manufacture and package a cassette may be less than $1.00. Talk about keeping the proper perspective! The record company is really watching their bottom line here, aren't they? They are also, unfortunately, very reluctant to negotiate this point, as most attorneys have discovered. It's a tough one, but you're probably going to have to live with it. That leaves a royalty base price (the price against which the royalty percentage rate is applied) of $8.78. The production company's royalty rate of 12% applied against the royalty base price means that the production company receives a royalty of $1.05 per cassette. In the case of the artist, whose royalty rate is 8% of the royalty base price, the royalty due per cassette will be 70¢.

As designated in paragraph 10(o) of the exclusive recording artist/production company contract, no royalties are payable in respect of records given away as free goods, provided the amounts do not exceed 200 nonroyalty-bearing LPs out of every 1,000 LPs distributed. Once again, the application of the correct "'rithmetic" formula will show that 20% of all cassettes shipped will be considered free goods and therefore deducted from the calculation of actual cassettes sold. In our case, where there are 100,000 cassettes shipped, that's 20,000 given away as free goods, leaving 80,000 cassettes which are considered sold for royalty calculation purposes.

So, now we can finally determine the royalties that are owed for cassettes, right? Not so fast. Paragraph 10q also states that the royalty will be paid on only ninety percent (90%) of the records sold; ninety percent (90%) of 80,000 units equals 72,000 cassettes for which royalties are payable. Finally, multiply the royalty ($1.05) per cassette for the production company and for the artist multiply $.70 by the number of royalty-bearing cassettes sold (72,000 units). This results in the production company earning $75,600 and the artist earning $50,400 in cassette royalties.

Now let's look at the royalties due the production company and artist for sales of CDs.

## CD ROYALTIES

| *Production CompanyRoyalties* | | | *Contract Para. #* | *Artist Royalties* |
|---|---|---|---|---|
| Royalties | | CDs | | |
| | $15.98 | Retail List Price | | |
| Less: | 4.00 | Packaging Deduction (25% of $15.98) | 10r(iii) | |
| | $11.98 | Royalty Base Price | | $11.98 Royalty Base Price |
| | x 9% | Production Co. Royalty Rate (75% of 12%) | 10g | x 6% Artist Royalty Rate (75% of 8%) |
| | $1.08 Royalty Per CD | | | $.72 Royalty Per CD |
| | * 200,000 CDs | | | |
| Less: | 40,000 | Free Goods | 10o | |
| | 160,000 CDs Sold | | | |
| Less: | 16,000 | (10% of 160,000) Breakage Deduction | | |

*continued*

| Production Company Royalties | Contract Para. # | Artist Royalties |
|---|---|---|
| 144,000 (90% of 160,000 Royalty Bearing CDs) x 1.08 Royalty per CD $155,520 CD Royalties | 10 | 144,000 (90% of 160,000 Royalty Bearing CDs) x $.72 Royalty per CD $103,680 CD Royalties |

In our example, the average retail list price of an LP in the CD configuration for a new artist is $15.98. Why is there such a big difference in the price of the CDs and cassettes, you might ask? Once again, the record company accountants and lawyers are trying to increase the profits received from the product. Remember, it is their job to maximize the value of their company.

Well, a brief look back will help us recall that when the CD was first introduced commercially on a widespread level in the early 1980s, the major record manufacturers and distributors justified a higher retail list price because of the high cost of researching and developing this new technology and building new plants to manufacture them. This argument may have been valid at the time. But, over the course of the past 20 years these costs have been more than offset many times over. Today a CD can be manufactured and packaged for a cost close to that of a cassette. In addition, the ratio of sales of CDs to cassettes is continuing to favor CDs, making the higher packaging deduction for CDs an important factor in the record company's profits. Recently, CD buyers and some record store owners have made claims that the major labels have conspired to unduly pressure retailers to keep the actual selling price of CDs above eleven dollars ($11.00) in order for the label to sustain their steep profit margins. As a result, these disgruntled parties allege the record buying public is being ripped off by a price-fixing scheme. Recently, most major labels have reached a settlement with the Federal Trade Commission (FTC) regarding these charges which require a change in the major labels' practices and may ultimately lead to a reduction in the actual selling price of CDs.

Just as in the case of the cassette configuration of the LP in paragraph 10r of the Exclusive Recording Artist/Production Company contract, a packaging deduction is taken "off the top" of the suggested $15.98 retail price before the CD royalty base price is determined. However, instead of the 20% container deduction formula used as with cassettes denoted in paragraph 10r, the container deduction for CDs is 25%. The CD container deduction of four dollars ($4.00) is more than four (4) times the actual cost of manufacturing and packaging the product. As you can see, the application of the packaging deduction to the retail selling price results in a $11.98 CD royalty base price.

If you thought that was bad, just wait until you hear this. You might recall my taking note of the reduced royalty rate for CDs as contained in paragraph 10g of the recording artist/production company contract. This paragraph states, that "with respect to records in compact disc form, . . . the royalty rate . . . shall be seventy-five percent (75%) of the . . . Basic U.S. LP Rate." So, as a result of this provision, instead of a royalty of 12% for the production company and 8% for the artist, the royalty rates are reduced to 9% for the production company and 6% for the artist. I'm sure you have noticed the large display for CDs in record stores as opposed to the minute section for cassettes. The preceding breakdown should make it easy for you to understand why the major distributors are doing all they can to promote the sale of CDs rather than the sale of cassettes.

In watching the flow of money through the contract, you can see that the record companies are winning on both fronts. They're making sure retailers are charging the public more for CDs while paying production companies and artists about the same royalties for CDs as they do for cassettes. In this statement of recording earnings, the production company is getting only $1.08 for CDs as opposed to $1.05 for cassette LPs. The artist earns only 72¢ per CD LP as opposed to 70¢ per cassette LP.

After the 20% free goods and 10% breakage deductions, the number of royalty-bearing CDs is 144,000. When you multiply that number by the per CD royalty rate, it results in the production company being entitled to $155,520 in royalties and the artist, $103,680.

The total royalties earned for the LP in both cassette and CD configurations would be as follows:

| *Production Company* | | *Artist* | |
|---|---|---|---|
| TOTAL CASSETTE AND CD ROYALTIES | | | |
| 75,600 | Cassette Royalties | 50,400 | Cassette Royalties |
| +155,520 | CD Royalties | +103,680 | CD Royalties |
| $ 231,120 | Total Royalties Earned by Production Co. | $154,080 | Total Royalties Earned by Artist |

While these royalties may have been earned by the production company and the artist, it is not necessarily the amount payable to each of them. The amount due each party will depend upon the terms of their agreements. In the case of the production company, it will be based on its deal with the major record distributor; in the case of the artist, it's determined by the exclusive recording artist contract with the production company.

**Keep in mind that the distributor must account to the production company by submitting a royalty statement.**

As indicated earlier, based on the assumption that the production company's contract with the major record distributor is an "all-in" deal, the production company is responsible for payment of the advances and royalties due the artist according to its exclusive recording artist contract.

Now let's take a look at a sample royalty statement for the production company and artist. Keep in mind that the distributor must account to the production company by submitting a royalty statement. The production company, in turn (according to the exclusive recording artist contract), is also obligated to submit a royalty statement to the artist. Be sure to also note the difference in monies deducted from royalties due the artist, as a result of the video and independent promotion cost recoupment provisions contained in the exclusive recording artist contract between the artist and production company, as opposed to the more favorable provision assumed in the production company/distributor contract.

## SAMPLE ROYALTY STATEMENT

| *Production Company Royalties* | | *Contract Para.#* | *Artist Royalties* | |
|---|---|---|---|---|
| $ 231,120 | Total Royalties Earned by Production Co. | | $ 154,080 | Total Royalties Earned by Artist |
| –57,780 | Reserve (25% of $231,120) | 12. | $–100,000 | Recording Costs |
| –250,000 | Advance from Distributor | | –38,520 | Reserve (25% of $154,080) |
| | | | –20,000 | Artist Advance from Production Company |
| –30,000 | Video Costs (50% of $60,000) | 15. | –60,000 | Video Costs (100% of $60,000) |
| –25,000 | Independent Promotion Costs (50% of $50,000) | 2.a. | –50,000 | Independent Promo Costs (100% of $50,000) |
| **$–131,660** | Unrecouped Balance With Distributor | | **$–114,440** | Unrecouped Balance with Production Company |

Before reading any farther, take a moment to review paragraph 12 of the exclusive recording artist contract. It states that the "company will retain a reserve against all payable royalties." Some distributors may retain reserves of up to fifty percent (50%) of royalties due new artists, in order to be protected from paying royalties on records that could eventually be returned by retailers for credit. In other words, the distributor is concerned that approximately one-half of the records shipped could be returned and therefore royalties won't be payable for these records.

In our sample statement, a twenty-five percent (25%) reserve is imposed. As you can see, in the statement due the production company, $57,760 is automatically deducted from the production company royalties for reserves, while the statement from the production company to the artist shows a deduction of $38,520 for reserves from the royalties due the artist.

Advances are the next amounts deducted from the earned royalties. The distributor deducts (or recoups) the $250,000 advance it paid to the production company while the production company, in its statement to the artist, deducts (recoups) the $20,000 it advanced to the artist.

Next, according to paragraph 15a of the exclusive recording artist contract, one hundred percent (100%) of video costs are recoupable from all royalties due the artist. This means, in the case of the artist's statement, that the entire $60,000 in video costs are deducted from the earned royalties. Paragraph 2(a) of the contract also allows the production company to recoup one hundred percent (100%) of all independent promotion costs or $50,000. This is also an unusually high percentage; normally only fifty percent (50%) of such costs are recoupable. It is assumed that the distributor/production company contract allows the recoupment of only fifty percent (50%) of video costs of $60,000 and independent promotion costs of $50,000. Therefore, only $30,000 and $25,000 of these respective costs are deducted from the production company's royalties.

It's very important to note what the potential difference would be in royalties owed the artist if the video and independent promotion costs had been only 50% instead of 100% recoupable. Had the recoupment basis of these two costs been 50% instead of 100%, the artist account would have been unrecouped only $59,440. Instead, after deduction of reserves, advances, and various costs, the production company's account has an unrecouped balance of –$131,660 and the artist's account an unrecouped balance of –$114,440. Now you can see why even an artist that achieves a gold record (500,000 units in sales) may earn little, if any, money from record royalties. However, the production company and artist *may* generate more income from the additional advances they might obtain for recording a second LP. That, of course, will depend on whether the distributor exercises its option (if it has one) in its agreement with the production company. But, even in today's competitive market, the sales of 300,000 units of a debut LP of a relatively unknown artist, as is the case here, may be considered a good indicator of the possibility of even greater sales of the artist's follow-up LP. So, it is likely that the distributor would, in a case such as this, exercise its option to have the production company record a second LP for an advance of, let's say, $275,000, which assumes $25,000 escalation from the first LPs recording fund advance paid to the production company. If so, the production company would in turn, exercise its option to extend the term of the exclusive recording artist contract and, pursuant to the terms of that agreement, the artist would be entitled to an additional artist advance of $15,000 for the second LP, which amount is greater than that which would be due pursuant to the min/max advance formula contained in paragraph 7(d)(1) of the contract. I'm sure you're wondering, as did I, when I first reviewed this contract, why the artist's attorney (who wasn't me) allowed the minimum artist advance for the second LP to be lower than that due for the 1st LP. This is very unusual in that artist advances for subsequent LP routinely escalate at least $10–$25,000 from the amount of the immediately preceding LP.

As a result of the restrictive terms of recoupment of more and more costs associated with the recording and promotion of the product, it is becoming increasingly difficult for the production company and the artists to generate significant royalties from recording. It has therefore become increasingly more important for production companies and artists to realize earnings from owning their copyrights. The next section delves deeper into the true "money-maker" in the music industry.

8

# Copyright Principles

## *The Copyright "Bundle of Rights"*

The copyright is the most valuable asset in the music business. That's right! *The most valuable asset.* I want to reiterate that the goals of a successful production company should include the procurement and exploitation of as many copyrights as possible. This needs to be done because after the delivery of five to eight LPs by an artist, the production company's contractual rights to the services of the artist under an exclusive recording agreement will eventually end. In most cases, the record company, rather than the production company, owns the masters and, as a result reaps the benefits of the continued reuse of the masters. While I firmly believe that the production company should strive to maintain ownership of the masters, the master recordings will eventually reach the exploitation saturation point but the copyright of the composition embodied on the master recordings live on years after all of these other rights are gone.

Did you ever wonder why Motown Record Company was sold in 1988 for $84 million? One reason was that in the years immediately preceding the sale, Motown incurred significant expenses in simply keeping its large business operation afloat. Some industry insiders considered the selling price a paltry sum but it was no paltry sum in my book. You would think that Motown, with over 100 number one hits during its thirty-plus-year span, must have been worth more than that, right? I did as well and decided to take a closer look at what Berry Gordy, Motown's owner, actually sold and doing so clarified the situation for me. Berry Gordy sold the name Motown, the rights to old and future Motown master recordings, and the contractual rights to aging artists whose most recent records hadn't been selling well. What wasn't publicized at the time of the sale was that Berry Gordy maintained his publishing companies, Jobete and Stone Diamond, the entities which hold the ownership interests in thousands of valuable copyrights of the compositions contained on the master recordings which were sold. Many of us in the industry suspected that the value of those publishing interests exceeded that of the record label which he sold, and we were right. In the summer of 1997 it was announced that Berry Gordy had sold one-half (1/2) of his interest in his publishing companies for $125 million to EMI Publishing.

**So, what is this most valuable asset, the copyright? Well, first of all, the copyright isn't just one right, it's actually what many people describe as a "bundle," or a number of exclusive rights.**

Emerging production publishing companies should learn the following lessons from this story: (1) get the copyrights; (2) increase the value of the copyrights by promoting the recording of the songs (remember, Berry Gordy had a hundred number one hits); and (3) hold on to the copyrights.

So, what is this most valuable asset, the copyright? Well, first of all, the copyright isn't just one right, it's actually what many people describe as a "bundle," or a number of exclusive rights. The copyright, or the right to copy, is an intangible property right granted by statute to authors for the protection of their works. The best way to protect an author's work is to register it with the U.S. Copyright Office. Registration can be accomplished by filing a PA (performing arts) form for published or unpublished musical works or an SR (sound recording) form for sound recordings. If the same copyright claimant desires to protect the sound recording as well as the underlying musical work, only an SR form needs to be filed. The PA form of registration protects the underlying musical work while the SR form protects the sound recording. Both forms of registration give the owner certain statutory remedies, such as three times the provable damages and payment of the owner's attorney's fees by the party infringing on the work. These remedies are unavailable to a work that is unregistered. While, in some circumstances, certain unpublished works may be protected by a particular state's common law, authors are urged to pursue protection of their works by registering with the Register of Copyright Office. In order to complete the registration process, the following should be sent to the U.S. Copyright Office: (1) a copy of a phonorecord (CD or tape of the work if the work is unpublished; two copies, if it is published); (2) a PA or SR registration form; (3) a registration fee (currently $30.00).

There are four primary rights of the copyright "bundle of rights" that I am called upon by my clients to protect on a regular basis. These rights are: the mechanical right, the performance right, the synchronization right, and the derivative right.

***First is the mechanical right.*** This is the right to mechanically reproduce the musical work. A mechanical reproduction can be a cassette, a vinyl record, a CD, or other such reproduction of the musical work. In order to encourage the ability for one to record and distribute copyrighted works, the copyright law established a compulsory mechanical license. This license operates to establish a set royalty which must be paid to the copyright owner of the composition for the mechanical reproduction, manufacturing, and distribution of copies of the work. Effective January 1, 1998, the minimum compulsory mechanical royalty rate was increased to 7.1¢ and was increased on January 1, 2000, to 7.55¢, with further incremental increases on January 1 of even years through 2006.

Therefore, if a production company desires to record a composition written by a writer not affiliated with the production company and without an agreement to the contrary, it or the manufacturer of the CD or cassette (usually the record company) must pay the owner of the copyright of the composition the full compulsory mechanical royalty rate of 7.55¢ per mechanical reproduction of the work, in order not to infringe upon the copyright. In accordance with the law, a royalty of 7.55¢ must be paid for each mechanical reproduction of the composition, whether it is a long playing CD, a vinyl LP, a cassette single or CD of the composition. Considering the amount earned for each use, it's easy to see why this right is so important and valuable.

Suppose an artist who also happens to be a songwriter exclusively signed to the production company writes all ten (10) of the compositions on his or her CD. If the production company's publishing affiliate owns the copyrights of all the compositions, and the full mechanical royalty rate is paid for their use, the publishing company would be entitled to 75.5¢ in mechanical royalties for each long-playing CD. If 100,000 CDs are manufactured and distributed, the publishing company would be entitled to $75,500 in mechanical royalties. And just suppose that two of the compositions contained on the long playing CD are released on two separate CD or cassette singles that are certified gold by the RIAA (representing the sale of at least 250,000 copies) and generate $18,875 each. That's a total of $113,250 in mechanical royalties from the sale of LPs and singles.

Sounds like the way to amass a gold mine, huh? Well, I hate to burst your bubble, but most record companies obviously started to believe they were paying copyright owners a "gold mine" worth of royalties. So they began incorporating what has come to be known as *the controlled composition clause* in most artist and production company contracts. The controlled composition clause specifies that any compositions owned or controlled by the artist or production company must be licensed to the record company at three-quarters (¾) of the statutory compulsory minimum mechanical royalty rate. So, instead of being paid 7.55¢ per copy, the copyright owner is paid three-quarters (¾) of that amount or roughly 5¢ per copy of the composition. In the previous example, if the terms of a controlled composition clause were applied, the total royalties owed to the copyright owner would be reduced to roughly $84,937.50. The record company's rationale for needing a controlled composition clause is that, by investing in the recording, manufacture, promotion, and distribution of the record, it should be "cut a break" in having to pay the full mechanical royalty rate. My advice to the artist or production company who has enough clout is to try to get the record company to agree to pay a higher percentage or the full statutory minimum mechanical royalty rate.

It is important to note that if the production company decides to manufacture and release its own product, it is also subject to paying mechanical royalties to the owners of copyrights of the works contained on the CDs or cassettes. Again, the production company owner has to recognize that when he or she manufactures, sells, and gets paid for the product, all the money he or she receives is not for him or her. Not only does the production company have to pay artist and producer royalties, it also has to pay mechanical royalties to the copyright owners.

***Next is the performance right*** or the right to publicly perform the musical work. This right is usually licensed through the copyright owner's performance right affiliate. Affiliating as a publishing company and songwriter with one of the major performance rights organization's (ASCAP, BMI, or SESAC) is the best way to exploit this right. As I always say, "whenever the music is played somebody gets paid." These organizations are national organizations qualified and staffed to best protect and exploit a copyright owner's rights in this area. ASCAP, BMI, and Sesac operate on the basis that they each control a significant number of the copyrights publicly performed on radio and television stations, in venues, or wherever music is performed across the nation. As a result, they have considerable leverage in convincing radio stations, television stations, restaurants, clubs, and other users to pay annual fees for the right to use, or publicly perform, any of the works contained in the respective organization's catalog of works of affiliated publishers and songwriters. Each of the three organizations aggressively markets itself as the best performance rights organization for songwriters and publishers to be affiliated with in order to receive the maximum royalties from the licensing of these rights. ASCAP, BMI, and SESAC each have their own system of tracking and calculating the amount of money each performed composition earns.

Prior to 1990, many experts, including myself, concluded that BMI was more thorough in canvassing black radio stations and therefore paid larger royalties to owners of copyrights targeted to the black audience. However, over the past ten (10) years ASCAP has revamped its system and is currently believed to pay higher royalties in most genres of music. In response to ASCAPs revised system, BMI has also revised its tracking and payment methods in an effort to maintain current members as well as lure new members. In either case, there is a substantial difference in the amounts of royalties paid for records which appear on the pop charts as opposed to those on the R&B or country charts. For example, a composition contained on a record that reaches number one on the pop charts may generate 5 to 10 times the earnings of a composition that just tops the R&B or country chart. Another important point to remember is that the royalties earned as a result of licensing the performance rights are based on the number of public performances of the work, not on record sales. If you have a rap record that has sold a half million units with very little, if any, radio play, do not expect a significant royalty check from your performance rights organization. Most of the royalties are paid to copyright owners whose compositions are played on the radio and are therefore "tracked" so as to trigger royalty payments. However, for a highly charted record that is both selling well and being played on a lot of radio stations, the performance right will usually be the runner-up to the mechanical right as a primary source of income to the copyright owner.

***Another part of the bundle is the synchronization right.*** This is the right to synchronize the work from one medium to another and primarily covers situations where a master recording of a copyrighted work is "synchronized" or "made a part of" another product, such as a movie, television program, or commercial. When this is done, the user of the prior copyrighted work must obtain the right to incorporate the copyrighted work into the new product from the copyright owner. This right is usually licensed by the copyright owner to the user directly by means of a license agreement. The terms of such a license may vary. In the case where a previously recorded master recording of a copyrighted work is synchronized into a movie, the movie production company may attempt to "buy out" (pay a one-time flat fee) for the right to use the work for all purposes. However, depending on the copyright owner's leverage, I would attempt to negotiate a separate fee for the various forms of exploitation of the movie such as its feature film release, video cassette release, and cable or network and international showings.

In some circumstances, where a movie company requests the creation of a composition for both synchronization in the movie and the movie's sound track, the movie company may demand to co-publish or participate in owning up to 50% of the work. This may be a tough point for the copyright owner to swallow. But, considering a movie company's considerable power to expose the composition, this proposal may have to be accepted in order to "jump start" the exploitation of a composition.

***Last is the derivative right.*** This is the right to derive a new work from a prior copyrighted work. Years ago, the movie *Harper Valley PTA* was inspired by and based on a previously copyrighted composition of the same name. In order for the new work, *Harper Valley PTA* the movie, not to infringe on the copyright of the composition, the producers of the movie were required to obtain a license from the owner of the composition in order to base the movie on the lyrics of the composition. In the late 1980s, a movie entitled *Lean On Me* used a version of the hit composition previously written and made popular by Bill Withers in 1972. The use of the song as the title of the movie gave rise to the need for the movie's producers to obtain a license from the copyright owners of the composition. While these are examples of the derivative right, the use of samples of copyrighted works in new works has promulgated the newest and most complex set of issues regarding the derivative right.

Don't sample! (or be sure to obtain the clearance to use a copyrighted work before you do).

In an article I wrote for *Agent & Manager* magazine in the early

1990s, I warned: "Rap Managers Beware: Sampling Can Be Hazardous to Your Financial Health." In that article I noted how the use of samples enriched the owners of the sampled copyrights while decreasing earnings to the samplers. Well, sampling still occurs and has some financial results for all concerned. Today, better systems are established to help clear the use of copyrights, but in order to clear it, you first have to know what a "sample" is.

The technical definition of sampling is the electronic digital lifting of portions ("samples") of a previously recorded work for insertion in a new master recording. This form of creating derivative works based on prior copyrights came into prominence with the emergence of the rap era that began in the late 1970s. Some of the first popular rap recordings like "Rappers Delight" used the entire rhythm track of the song, "Good Times," previously written by Niles Rodgers and Bernard Edwards, and recorded by members of their group Chic. While the technical definition of sampling requires the lifting and subsequent use of a portion of a prior master recording, the term has also been used to describe the use of a prior copyrighted melody in a new master recording. Although this practice isn't technically considered "sampling," it does raise the same issue of infringing on the copyright of a prior copyrighted composition.

At this point, I think a definition of the term *copyright claimant* as well as an explanation of the difference between a PR and an SR form of copyright registration is in order. As I stated previously, under the law of most states, authors of original works may be able to claim common law copyright protection for their work if it can be proved that they are the originator of the work. The best form of protection can be had by filing a PR form with the U.S. Copyright Office. The PR form of copyright registration operates to protect the owner of the composition from copyright infringement. While the PR type of copyright registration protects the underlying composition, the SR form of copyright registration protects the actual mechanical reproduction of the composition from infringement. The manufacturer of the recording, usually the record company, owns the sound recording copyright, which gives it remedies should bootleggers copy or duplicate it or various parts of the recording.

In a true case of sampling, where the master recording of a composition is digitally made a part of a subsequent new recording, derivative rights must be obtained by the party using the sample from the owners of both the composition and the master recording in order to avoid a potential copyright infringement claim. The new work may be a derivative of the copyright of the composition (owned by the author or publisher and protected by a PR registration) and/or the master recording (owned by the record manufacturer and protected by an SR registration).

It would be best to avoid copyright infringement by obtaining permission from the owner of the work prior to using the work. This is usually achieved by obtaining a license or clearance agreement from the owner in exchange for some form of monetary consideration. This can be a flat buyout fee for the right to use the works in all mediums or a royalty of some sort.

The smart songwriter or production company owner who is capable of creating or attracting creators of powerful product will build greater value and worth in his or her company by not having to share mechanical, performance, and other royalties with the other copyright owners. To further expound on the monetary effect of using samples, you only have to consider the controlled composition clause contained in most production company agreements with record companies, where the record company is already paying the production company three-quarters (¾) of the minimum statutory mechanical royalty rate or roughly five cents (5¢) rather than seven cents per mechanical reproduction. If your production company achieves a gold record (500,000 units sold), of which just one track contains a melody of a prior copyright-protected composition, the owner of this copyright may demand that you split the copyright to the newly created work with them on a 50-50 basis. Instead of five cents (5¢) per copy, you've just reduced your earnings to two and a half cents (2.5¢) per copy, a substantial difference to your bottom line.

My warning to songwriters or production company owners looking to maximize their company's worth by developing a strong publishing company owning a significant number of copyrights: Don't sample! Don't sample! Don't (and I mean, *Don't*) sample!

If after that, however, you don't take my advice or just can't help sampling, be sure you obtain a clearance to use the sampled work from one of the sample clearance "houses," as they're called. These small but effective operations will, for a fee, track down the owners of the sampled work and obtain a license agreement for the work's use. Usually these rights are obtained for an advance, which could run into thousands of dollars and may be recouped against an agreed-upon royalty. In some cases, the owner of the infringed-upon work may demand a percentage interest in the ownership of the new work.

Keep the proper perspective in mind. If you hope to build a strong base in the most important asset in the music business, and you, or your company's songwriter-producers are creative enough, I would urge you to maximize your creativity and your assets by not sampling! Remember, maximizing your creativity results in maximizing your assets.

While it's important to remember there are other lesser rights that are also part of the copyright "bundle of rights," the mechanical, performance, synchronization, and derivative rights are the key rights that result in generating the bulk of income for songwriters or production companies in today's popular music.

The following exclusive songwriter and co-publishing and administration contracts more fully explain the relationship between the songwriter and co-publishers.

# 9

# Exclusive Songwriter Contract

## *Analysis of Songwriter/Publishing Company Agreement*

### GRANTING COPYRIGHTS

**CONTRACT**

**Exclusive Songwriter Agreement**

THIS AGREEMENT made and entered into this ____ day of ________________, ___, by and between [Name of Production Company's Publishing Company], individually and as Administrator and Co-publisher for [Songwriter/Artist's Name] and/or his publishing designee with offices located at [Address of Production Company's Publishing Company] (hereinafter

**ANALYSIS**

**Analysis of Exclusive Songwriter Agreement**

This Agreement, between the production company's publishing company and artist's publishing company (jointly referred to as publishers) and the artist covers his or her exclusive services as a songwriter during the term, which is coterminous with the exclusive recording agreement.

**CONTRACT**

**referred to as "Publishers") and [Songwriter/Artist's Name and Address] (hereinafter referred to as "Writer").**

**WITNESSETH**

**WHEREAS, publisher, [Name of Production Company's Publishing Company] its affiliate [Name of Production Company] and [Name of Production Company's Management Company] have entered into a Co-Publishing, Exclusive Recording (hereinafter "Recording Agreement") and Personal Management Agreement respectively, with Writer or Writer's Publishing Designee of even date and it is hereby the intention of the parties that the term hereof shall be coterminous with the term of the Exclusive Recording Agreement;**

**NOW, THEREFORE, for good and valuable consideration the receipt of which is hereby acknowledged by each party hereto, it is agreed as follows:**

**1. EMPLOYMENT. Publisher hereby employs Writer to render Writer's services as a songwriter and composer and otherwise as may hereinafter be set forth. Writer hereby accepts such employment and agrees to render such services exclusively for Publisher during the term hereof, upon the terms and conditions set forth herein.**

**ANALYSIS**

1. Under this agreement, the artist/songwriter is purposely deemed an employee of the publishers which gives the publisher the benefit of a prolonged period of ownership of the copyrights written during the term. This concept is more fully explained in the analysis of paragraph 6A of this Agreement.

**CONTRACT**

2. TERM. The initial term of this agreement shall commence upon the date hereof and continue for the initial term of the Recording Agreement. It is the intention of the parties hereto that the term hereof shall be coterminous with the term of the Recording Agreement (a copy of the pertinent part thereof is hereby attached hereto and incorporated herein and marked as attachment "A"), as same may be renewed or extended from time to time. Accordingly, each extension or renewal of the term of the Recording Agreement shall automatically extend or renew the term hereof for the same period. The phrase "the term hereof" or "the term of this agreement" as used in this agreement, shall refer to the initial and any extension or renewal terms hereof in accordance with the foregoing. Notwithstanding anything to the contrary contained herein, in the event either the Management, Co-Publishing or Songwriters Agreements are terminated for any reason prior to the end of that term of the Recording Agreement, all of the agreements between the parties shall be terminated at that time.

3. GRANT OF RIGHTS. Writer hereby irrevocably and absolutely assigns, conveys and grants to Publisher, its successors and assigns (a) all rights and interests of every kind, nature and description in and to all original musical compositions and all original arrange-

**ANALYSIS**

3. During the term of the Agreement, the artist grants and assigns all rights and interests, in the copyrights written, to the publishers including the right to:

**CONTRACT** | **ANALYSIS**

ments of musical compositions in the public domain which have heretofore been written, composed or created by Writer, in whole or in part, alone or in collaboration with others, including but not limited to the titles, lyrics and music thereof and all world-wide copyrights and renewals and extensions thereof under the present or future laws throughout the world, to the extent any of the foregoing shall not heretofore have been conveyed by Writer to an unrelated third party; and (b) all rights and interests of every kind, nature and description in and to the results and proceeds of Writer's services hereunder, including but not limited to the titles, lyrics and music of all original musical compositions and of all original arrangements of musical compositions in the public domain and all universe-wide copyrights and renewals and extensions thereof under any present or future laws throughout the world, which shall be written, composed or created by Writer during the term hereof, in whole or in part, alone or in collaboration with others; and (c) all rights and interests of every kind, nature and description in and to all original musical compositions and all original arrangements of musical compositions in the public domain which are now directly or indirectly owned or controlled by Writer, in whole or in part, along or with others, or the direct or indirect ownership or control of which shall be

**CONTRACT**

acquired, by Writer during the term hereof, in whole or in part, alone or with others, as the employer or transferee of the writers or composers thereof or otherwise, including the titles, lyrics and music thereof and all universe-wide copyrights and renewals and extensions thereof under any present or future laws throughout the universe; all of which musical compositions, arrangements, rights and interests Writer hereby warrants and represents are and shall at all times be Publisher's exclusive property as the sole owner thereof, free from any adverse claims or rights therein by any other party (all such musical compositions and arrangements hereinafter being referred to as "Compositions").

Without limiting the generality of the foregoing, Writer acknowledges that the rights and interests hereinabove set forth include Writer's irrevocable grant to Publisher, its successors and assigns, of the sole and exclusive right, license, privilege and authority throughout the entire universe with respect to all Compositions, whether now in existence or whether created during the term hereof, as follows:

(a) To exploit and license others to perform through sound recordings the Compositions publicly or privately, for profit or otherwise, by means of public or private performance, radio broadcast, television, or any and all other means of me-

**ANALYSIS**

(a) exploit and license the compositions in all media and by any means;

| CONTRACT | ANALYSIS |
| --- | --- |
| dia, whether now known or hereafter conceived or developed. | |
| (b) To substitute a new title or titles for the Compositions or any of them and to make any arrangement, adaptation, translation, dramatization or transposition of any or all of the Compositions or of the titles, lyrics or music thereof, in whole or in part, and in connection with any other musical, literary or dramatic material, and to add new lyrics to the music of any Compositions or new music to the lyrics of any Composition, all as Publisher may deem necessary or desirable in its best business judgment. | (b) substitute or change the title, lyrics or music contained in the composition; |
| (c) To secure copyright registration and protection of the Compositions in Publisher's or it's designee's name or otherwise, as Publisher may desire, at Publisher's own cost and expense, and at Publisher's election, including any and all renewals and extensions of copyright under any present or future laws throughout the universe, and to have and to hold said copyrights, renewals and extensions and all rights existing thereunder, for and during the full term of all said copyrights and all renewals and extensions and all rights existing thereunder, for and during the full term of all said copyrights and all renewals and extensions thereof. | (c) secure copyright registration in the publisher's name; |
| (d) To make or cause to be made, and to license others to | (d) license for mechanical, synchronized use, etc.; |

**CONTRACT**

make master records, transcriptions, soundtracks, processing and any other mechanical, electrical or other reproductions of the compositions, in whole or in part, in such form or manner and as frequently as Publisher shall determine, including the right to synchronize the Compositions with sound motion pictures and to use, manufacture, advertise, license or sell such reproductions for any and all purposes, including without limitation private and public performances, radio broadcast, television, and motion picture, wired radio, phonograph records and any and all other means or devices, whether now known or hereafter conceived or developed.

(e) To print, publish and sell, and to license others to print, publish and sell, sheet music, orchestrations, arrangements and other editions of the Compositions in all forms, including, without limitation, the inclusion of any or all of the Compositions in song folios, compilations, song books, mixed folios, personality folios and lyric magazines with or without music.

(f) Any and all other rights now or hereafter existing in all Compositions under and by virtue of any common law rights and all copyrights and renewals and extensions thereof including so-called small performance rights. Writer grants to Publisher, without any compensation other than as specified

**ANALYSIS**

(e) print or otherwise publish the song's music and/or lyrics;

(f) use the artist's name and likeness for purposes of the exploitation of the works;

The artist/songwriter also warrants and represents that he or she has the full right and power to fulfill the terms of the contract, and in no way will the performance of the contract infringe on the rights of others. This

| CONTRACT | ANALYSIS |
|---|---|
| herein, the perpetual right to use and publish and to permit others to use and publish Writer's name (including any professional name heretofore or hereafter adopted by Writer), Writer's photograph or other likeness, or any reproduction or simulation thereof, and biographical material concerning Writer, and the titles of any and all of the Compositions, in connection with the printing, sale, advertising, performance, distribution and other exploitation of the Compositions, and for any other purpose related to the business of Publisher, its affiliated and related companies, or to refrain therefrom. This right shall be exclusive during the term hereof and nonexclusive thereafter. Writer shall not authorize or permit the use of Writer's name or likeness, or any reproduction or simulation thereof, or biographical material concerning Writer, for or in connection with any musical compositions, other than by or for Publisher. Writer grants Publisher the right to refer to Writer as Publisher's "Exclusive Songwriter and Composer" or to use any other similar and appropriate appellation, during the term hereof.<br><br>4. EXCLUSIVITY. During the term of this agreement, Writer shall not write or compose, or furnish or convey, any musical compositions, titles, lyrics, or music, or any rights or interests therein, nor participate in any manner with regard to same, for or to any party | provision is very important to the publishers because it requires the songwriter to guarantee that he or she has not entered into an agreement with another party, such as a competing publisher, which would interfere with his or her performance of this contract.<br><br>This grant of rights provision is very broad and should be a cause of concern for the songwriter. On behalf of the songwriter, I would demand certain limits be placed on the publishers rights to change or alter the compositions, exploit the compositions by any means, and the use of the artist's name.<br><br>A recognizable and memorable example of why the songwriter should want to limit the publisher's right to change or alter the lyrics of a composition occurred during the 1996 presidential campaign. At some of the campaign stops of presidential candidate Bob Dole, the lyrics of the hook of the hit song, "Soul Man," were sung as "I'm a Dole Man." Isaac Hayes, one of the writers of the original song, objected to the use of the tune in this manner. But under the terms of this agreement, a songwriter would forfeit their right to object to the publisher's approval of such an alteration of the lyrics.<br><br>In situations where I have represented songwriters, I have been able to negotiate limits on this type of provision by requiring the publishers to first obtain the consent of the songwriter for potentially objectionable uses such as this. |

**CONTRACT**

other than Publisher, nor permit the use of his name or likeness as the writer or co-writer of any musical composition by any party other than Publisher.

5. WARRANTIES, REPRESENTATIONS, COVENANTS AND AGREEMENTS. Writer hereby warrants, represents, covenants and agrees as follows: Writer has the full right, power and authority to enter into and perform this Agreement and to grant to and vest in Publisher all rights herein set forth, free and clear of any and all claims, rights and obligations whatsoever; all of the Compositions and all other results and proceeds of the services of Writer hereunder, including all of the titles, lyrics and music of the Compositions and each and every part thereof, delivered and to be delivered by Writer hereunder are and shall be new and original and capable of copyright protection throughout the entire world; no Composition shall, either in whole or in part, be an imitation or copy of, or infringe upon, any other material, or violate or infringe upon any common law or statutory rights of any party including, without limitation, contractual rights, copyrights and rights of privacy; and Writer has not sold, assigned, leased, licensed or in any other way disposed of or encumbered any Composition, in whole or in part, or any rights herein granted to Publisher, nor shall Writer sell, as-

**ANALYSIS**

**CONTRACT**

**sign, lease, license or in any other way dispose of or encumber any of the Compositions, in whole or in part, or any of said rights, except under the terms and conditions hereof.**

**6. POWER OF ATTORNEY. Writer hereby irrevocably constitutes, authorizes, empowers and appoints Publisher or any of its officers Writer's true and lawful attorney (with full power of substitution and delegation), in Writer's name, and in Writer's place and stead, or in Publisher's name, to take and do such action, and to make, sign, execute, acknowledge and deliver any and all instruments or documents, which Publisher from time to time may deem desirable or necessary to vest in Publisher, its successors and assigns, all of the rights or interests granted by Writer hereunder, including without limitation, such documents as Publisher, its successors and assigns, the worldwide copyrights for all compositions for the entire term of copyright and for any and all renewals and extensions under any present or future laws throughout the universe. Notwithstanding the foregoing, Writer acknowledges that he (or she) is Publisher's employee for hire, and that Publisher is accordingly the author of all Compositions for all purposes of the 1909 or 1976 Copyright Law or any succeeding Copyright Law.**

**ANALYSIS**

6. A Power of Attorney is granted from the artist to the publishers allowing the publishers to execute, sign or take such other action necessary to assign the rights granted therein to the publishers. The artist/songwriter also acknowledges that he or she is the publisher's employee for hire for copyright law purposes.

Under copyright law, the copyright vests with the "author" of a work who is usually the writer. However, if the writer is writing as an employee and within the scope of his employment with the publisher, the publisher, not the writer, is deemed the "author". The very important aspect of this designation pertains to the length of time the ownership of a work may be retained by the publisher. For example, if the publisher is the employer of a writer for hire, it will retain the ownership of the work for the longer of 100 years from the date of creation of the work or 75 years from the date of publication of the work. If the writer is not designated an employee for hire, he or she is the author and the copyright in the work will vest in the author's name and will exist for the life of the author, plus 50 years. Moreover, if the writer is not working as an employee for hire for the publisher, the writer may

## CONTRACT

**7. COMPENSATION/ROYALTIES. Provided that Writer shall duly perform the terms, covenants and conditions of this agreement, Publisher shall pay Writer, for the services to be rendered by Writer hereunder and for the rights acquired and to be acquired by Publisher hereunder, the following compensation/royalties collected from a source on the Compositions:**

**(a) Ten cents ($.10) per copy for each copy of sheet music in standard piano/vocal notation and each dance orchestration printed, published and sold in the United States and Canada by Publisher or its licensees, for which payment shall have been received by Publisher, after deduction of returns.**

**(b) Ten percent (10%) of the wholesale selling price of each printed copy of each other arrangement and edition printed, published and sold in the United States and Canada by Publisher or its licensees, for which payment shall have been received by Publisher, after deduction of returns, except that in the event that any Compositions shall be used or caused to be used, in**

## ANALYSIS

grant the work to the publisher by way of a transfer or assignment and will have the right to terminate the transfer to the publisher between the 35th and 40th year after the execution of the grant or the date of first publication of the work. The right to terminate requires written notice to the publisher. However, because the designation of the writer as an employee may result in the publisher having to bear the responsibilities of extending the benefits of employment (workers' compensation insurance, unemployment insurance, etc.) most publishers are actually opting for the writer's assignment of the copyright rather than seeking the long term rights they could obtain by having the writer considered their employee.

7.(a) You might ask, "How is the songwriter compensated?" Well, this paragraph states that the songwriter will receive 10 cents per each copy of sheet music. The range for this royalty may vary from contract to contract from 5 cents to 12 cents or, in some rare cases, 50% of the publisher's receipts, which equals approximately 30 cents.

| **CONTRACT** | **ANALYSIS** |
|---|---|
| **whole or in part, in conjunction with one or more other musical compositions in a folio, compilation, song book or other publication, Writer shall be entitled to receive that proportion of the foregoing royalty which the number of Compositions contained therein shall bear to the total number of musical compositions therein.** | |
| **(c) Fifty percent (50%) of any and all net sums actually received (less any costs for collection) by Publisher in the United States from the exploitation in the United States and Canada by licensees of mechanical rights, grant rights, electrical transcription and reproduction rights, motion picture and television synchronization rights, dramatization rights and all other rights therein (except print rights, which are covered in (a) and (b) above, and public performance rights, which are covered in (d) below), whether or not such licensees are affiliated with, owned in whole or in part by, or controlled by Publisher.** | 7.(c) The songwriter is paid 50% of the net receipts collected by the publisher for the licensing of mechanical, synchronization and other use rights (except public performance). |
| **(d) Writer shall receive his public performance royalties throughout the world directly from the performing rights society with which he is affiliated, and shall have no claim whatsoever against Publisher for any royalties received by Publisher from any performing rights society which makes payment directly (or indirectly other than through Publisher) to Writer, authors and composers. If, how-** | 7.(d) The songwriter's portion of public performance royalties (50% of the amount allocated for the composition) is usually not collected by the publisher. It is instead paid from the performance rights organization (BMI, ASCAP, SESAC) directly to the writer. The publisher's portion is also paid direct to the publishers by the performance rights organizations and, in the case of a co-publishing arrangement, pursuant to an "Across the |

## CONTRACT

**ever, Publisher shall collect both the Writer's and Publisher's share of performance income directly and such income shall not be collected by Writer's public performance society, Publisher shall pay to Writer's fifty percent (50%) of all such net sums which are received by Publisher in the United States from the exploitation of such rights in the Compositions, throughout the world.**

**(e) Fifty percent (50%) of any and all net sums, after deduction of foreign taxes, actually received (less any costs of collection ) by Publisher in the United States from the exploitation of the Compositions in countries outside of the United States and Canada (other than public performance royalties, which are covered in (d) above), whether from collection agents, licensees, subpublishers or others, and whether or not same are affiliated with, owned in whole or in part by, or controlled by Publisher.**

**(f) Publisher shall not be required to pay any royalties on professional or complimentary printed sheet music copies which are distributed gratuitously to performing artists, orchestra leaders and disc jockeys or for advertising, promotional or exploitation purposes. Furthermore, no royalties shall be payable to Writer on consigned copies unless paid for, and not until such time as an accounting therefore can properly be made.**

## ANALYSIS

Board Deal", the songwriter's publishing company ("Participant") would be entitled to 50% of the publisher's share of 50% (or 25% of the whole), if the songwriter was the sole writer.

**CONTRACT**

(g) Royalties as hereinabove specified shall be payable solely to Writer in instances where Writer is the sole author of a Composition, including the lyrics and music thereof. However, in the event that one or more other songwriters are authors together with Writer of any Composition (including songwriters employed by Publisher to add, change or translate the lyrics or to revise or change the music), the foregoing royalties shall be divided equally among Writer and the other songwriters unless another division of royalties shall be agreed upon in writing between the parties concerned and timely written notice of such division is submitted to Publisher prior to payment.

(h) Except as herein expressly provided, no other royalties or monies shall be paid to Writer.

(i) Writer agrees and acknowledges that Publisher shall have the right to withhold from the royalties payable to Writer hereunder such amount, if any, as may be required under the provisions of all applicable Federal, State and other tax laws and regulations, and Writer agrees to execute such forms and other documents as may be required in connection therewith.

(j) In no event shall Writer be entitled to share in any advance payments, guarantee payments or minimum royalty payments which

**ANALYSIS**

**CONTRACT**

**Publisher shall receive in connection with any subpublishing agreement, collection agreement, licensing agreement or other agreement covering the Compositions or any of them.**

**8. ACCOUNTING. Publisher shall compute the royalties earned by Writer pursuant to this agreement between Writer and Publisher or its affiliates, whether now in existence or entered into at any time subsequent hereto, on or before March 31st for the semiannual period ending the preceding December 31st and on or before September 30th for the semiannual period ending the preceding June 30th, and shall thereupon submit to Writer the royalty statement for each such period together with the net amount of royalties, if any, which shall be payable after deducting any and all unrecouped advances and chargeable costs under this agreement or any other agreement. Each statement submitted by Publisher to Writer shall be binding upon Writer and not subject to any objection by Writer for any reason unless specific written objection, stating the basis thereof, is sent by Writer to Publisher within one (1) year after the date said statement is submitted. Writer or a certified public accountant on Writer's behalf may, at Writer's expense, at reasonable intervals (but not more frequent than once each year), examine Publisher's books insofar as same concern Writer,**

**ANALYSIS**

8. The Writer is accounted to on a semi-annual basis before March 31 and September 30 of each year for the sixth month period ending December 31st and June 30th. It's important to note that, in this Agreement, all unrecouped advances and costs under any and all other agreements may be recouped (cross collateralized) from royalties earned under this contract. Any objection by the writer to the accounting statements rendered must be made in writing before the end of one year after the receipt of the statement. The records of the publisher may be examined within two years after receipt of each statement by a representative who has been appointed by the writer.

**CONTRACT**

during Publisher's usual business hours and upon reasonable notice, for the purpose of verifying the accuracy of any statement submitted to Writer hereunder. Publisher's books relating to activities during any accounting period may only be examined as aforesaid during the two (2) year period following service by Publisher of the statement for said accounting period.

9. COLLABORATION. Whenever Writer shall collaborate with any other person in the creation of a Composition, the Composition shall be subject to the terms and conditions of this agreement, and Writer warrants, represents and agrees that prior to such collaboration Writer shall advise such other person of this exclusive agreement and shall further advise such other person that all Compositions so created must be published and owned by Publisher. In the event of any such collaboration, Writer shall notify Publisher of the nature and extent of such other person's contribution to the Composition, and Writer shall cause such other person to execute a separate songwriter's agreement with Publisher covering the Composition, which agreement shall set forth the division of the songwriter's royalties between Writer and such other person, and Publisher shall make payment accordingly.

10. SEPARATE AGREEMENTS. If Publisher so desires, Publisher

**ANALYSIS**

9. Suppose the writer collaborates with another writer in the composition of a song. Under the terms of this paragraph, the writer must inform such co-writer of the existence of this agreement and that the entire composition, including his or her contribution, shall be published by the publisher by way of a separate songwriters contract between the collaborator and publisher. While this provision can cause concern for a collaborator who is already signed with another publisher for the publishing of his or her works, it is an effective tool which enables the publisher to obtain valuable copyrights from new, unaffiliated writers who can collaborate with the publisher's more experienced writers.

10. In order to further document the Writer's share of each composi-

## CONTRACT

**may request Writer to execute a separate standard songwriters contract in Publisher's customary form with respect to each Composition hereunder. Upon such request, Writer shall promptly execute and deliver such separate agreement, and upon Writer's failure to do so, Publisher shall have the right, pursuant to the terms and conditions hereof, to execute such separate agreement on behalf of Writer. Such separate agreement shall supplement and not supersede this agreement. In the event of any conflict between the provisions of such separate agreement and this agreement, the provisions of this agreement shall govern. The failure of either of the parties hereto to execute such separate agreement, whether such execution is requested by Publisher or not, shall not affect the rights of each of the parties hereunder, including but not limited to the rights of Publisher to all of the Compositions written, composed or acquired by Writer during the term hereof.**

**11. WRITER'S SERVICES. (a) Writer shall perform his required services hereunder conscientiously, and solely and exclusively for and as requested by Publisher. Writer is a writer for hire hereunder, and all Compositions are acknowledged by Writer to be works made for hire. Writer shall duly comply with all requirements and requests made by Publisher in connection with its business as set forth herein. Writer**

## ANALYSIS

tion, the publisher may (and should) require the writer to execute a single song or separate songwriter's contract. This document is a valuable supplement to the Exclusive Songwriter Contract because it can: 1) serve as a separate document transferring the writer's copyrights of compositions to the publishers on a song by song basis; and 2) establish, in a writing executed by the parties, the agreement of multiple songwriters (if that is the case) as to their percentage of the songwriter's share of each composition. This provision goes further to grant the publisher the right to execute such an agreement on the writer's behalf should the writer fail to do so after being requested.

11. Do you remember my explanation of the reason for wanting the writer to compose on a work for hire basis for the publisher? From the historical perspective prior to the mid-70s, most songwriters had to sign exclusive songwriters agreements with publishers that didn't allow them to participate in copyright ownership at all. The songwriting duo, Ashford and Simpson, is an example of that. During their heyday of writing such hits as

**CONTRACT**

**shall deliver manuscript copy or tape copy of each Composition immediately upon the completion or acquisition of such Composition. Publisher shall use its reasonable efforts in its best business judgment to exploit any or all of said Compositions hereunder, but Publisher's failure to exploit said compositions shall not be deemed a breach hereof. Publisher at its sole discretion shall reasonably make studio facilities available for Writer so that Writer, subject to the supervision and control of Publisher, may produce demonstration records of the Compositions, and Writer shall have the right to perform at such recording sessions. Publisher shall also have the right to produce demonstration records hereunder. Writer shall not incur any liability for which Publisher shall be responsible in connection with any demonstration record session without having obtained Publisher's prior written approval as to the nature, extent and limit of such liability. In no event shall Writer incur any expense whatsoever on behalf of Publisher without having received prior written authorization from Publisher. Writer shall not be entitled to any compensation (except for such compensation as is otherwise provided for herein) with respect to services rendered in connection with any such demonstration recording sessions. Publisher shall advance the costs for the production of demon-**

**ANALYSIS**

"You're All I Need to Get By," "Ain't Nothing Like the Real Thing," and "Ain't No Mountain High Enough," they were employed as exclusive songwriters for the Motown affiliate, Jobete. Although Ashford and Simpson gave up any publishing interest in these songs (and any other compositions they created during the term of their agreement with Motown) they did obtain added benefits as a result of the magnificent on-going marketing and cross-promotion of the recordings of these great songs that Motown provided. It was recently reported that this hit songwriting duo were able to "get paid" as much as $25 million by issuing bonds, secured against payment of future songwriters royalties for these songs. Well, in this paragraph, under the heading Writer's Services, certain circumstances are detailed to, in essence, help further document the existence of the employer/employee relationship between the publisher and the writer. There are certain phrases which are intended to highlight the employer/publisher's control over the writer, such as:

- Writer shall perform as requested by publisher;
- Writer shall comply with all requirements and requests of publisher;
- Writer shall promptly deliver tape copies of compositions to publisher;
- Writer shall perform on and record demos pursuant to and under the direction and control of

**CONTRACT**

**stration records, subject to the foregoing, and one-half (1/2) of such costs shall be deemed additional advances to Writer hereunder and shall be recouped by Publisher from royalties payable to Writer by Publisher under this agreement or any other agreement between Writer and Publisher or its affiliates. All recordings and reproductions made at demonstration record sessions hereunder shall become the sole and exclusive property of Publisher, free of any claims whatsoever by Writer or any person deriving any rights from Writer.**

**(b) Writer shall, from time to time, at Publisher's reasonable request, and whenever same will not unreasonably interfere with prior professional engagements of Writer, appear for photography, artwork and other similar purposes under the direction of Publisher or its duly authorized agent, appear for interviews and other promotional purposes, and confer and consult with Publisher regarding Writer's services hereunder. Writer shall also cooperate with Publisher in promoting, publicizing and exploiting the Compositions and for any other purpose related to the business of Publisher. Writer shall not be entitled to any compensation (other than applicable union scale if appropriate) for rendering such services, but shall be entitled to reasonable transportation and living expenses if such expenses**

**ANALYSIS**

publisher (without compensation, I might add!);

- Writer shall bear half of the costs of the demos; said costs being recoupable from royalties;
- Writer shall appear for photographic and other sessions or promotional engagements (once again, without further compensation) at the request and direction of the publisher;

All of these requirements and acknowledgments on behalf of the writer, further support the publisher's contention that the compositions were composed by the writer on an employee for hire basis. This may entitle the publisher to retain the rights for the time prescribed under the copyright law regarding works created on a work for hire basis.

As mentioned earlier, most current publishers don't actually exert this type of control over their songwriter's activities and therefore opt for the songwriter to assign the copyright to them instead of being considered their employee for hire.

**CONTRACT** | **ANALYSIS**

must be incurred in order to render such services.

12. UNIQUE SERVICES. Writer acknowledges that the services to be rendered by Writer hereunder are of a special unique, unusual, extraordinary and intellectual character which gives them a peculiar value, the loss of which cannot be reasonably or adequately compensated in damages in an action at law, and that a breach by Writer of any of the provisions of this agreement will cause Publisher great and irreparable injury and damage. Writer expressly agrees that Publisher shall be entitled to the remedies of injunction and other equitable relief to enforce this agreement or to prevent a breach of this agreement or any provision hereof, which relief shall be in addition to any other remedies, for damages or otherwise, which may be available to Publisher.

13. ACTIONS. Publisher shall have the exclusive right to take such action as it deems necessary, either in Writer's name or its own name or in both names, against any party to protect all rights and interests acquired by Publisher hereunder. Writer, shall cooperate fully with Publisher in any controversy which may arise or litigation which may be brought concerning Publisher's rights and interests acquired hereunder. Publisher shall have the right, in its discretion, to

**CONTRACT**

employ attorneys and to institute or defend against any claim, action or proceeding, whether for infringement of copyright or otherwise, and to take any other necessary steps to protect the right, title and interest of Publisher in and to each Composition and, in connection therewith, to settle, compromise or in any other manner dispose of any such claim, action or proceeding and to satisfy or collect on any judgment which may be rendered. If Publisher shall recover on a judgment or as a result of a settlement with respect to any claim, action or proceeding for copyright infringement initiated by Publisher, all of Publisher's expenses in connection therewith, including, without limitation, attorney's fees and other costs, shall first be deducted, and fifty percent (50%) of the net proceeds shall be credited to Writer's account.

14. INDEMNITY. Writer hereby indemnifies, saves and holds Publisher, its successors and assigns, harmless from any and all liability, claims, demands, loss and damage (including counsel fees and court costs) arising out of or connected with any claim or action by a third party which is inconsistent with any of the warranties, representations or agreements by Writer in this agreement, and Writer shall reimburse Publisher, on demand, for any loss, cost, expense or damage to which said indemnity ap-

**ANALYSIS**

14. In this "indemnity" clause, the writer covers any losses sustained by the publisher for any breach of warranties by the writer. It is similar to the ones contained in the other agreements contained in this book. If the publishers receive a claim, the writer may participate in his/her defense at their own cost after receiving notice of the claim from the publisher. Pending the disposition of such a claim, the publishers may withhold any royalties due the writer in an amount reasonably related to the amount of the claim and the

**CONTRACT**

plies. Publisher shall give Writer prompt written notice of any claim or action covered by said indemnity, and Writer shall have the right, at Writer's expenses, to participate in the defense of any such claim or action with counsel of Writer's choice. Pending the disposition of any such claim or action, Publisher shall have the right to withhold payment of such portion of any monies which may be payable by Publisher to Writer under this agreement or under any other agreement between Writer and Publisher or its affiliates as shall be reasonably related to the amount of the claim and estimated counsel fees and costs. If Publisher shall settle or compromise any such claim or action, the foregoing indemnity shall cover only that portion (if any) of the settlement or compromise which shall have been approved in writing by Writer, and Writer hereby agrees not unreasonably to withhold any such approval. Notwithstanding the foregoing, if Writer shall withhold approval of any settlement or compromise which Publisher is willing to make upon advice of counsel and in its best business judgment, Writer shall thereupon deliver to Publisher an indemnity or surety bond, in a form satisfactory to Publisher, which shall cover the amount of the claim and estimated counsel fees and costs, and if Writer shall fail to deliver such bond within ten (10) business days,

**ANALYSIS**

estimated legal fees it will take to proceed with the case.

**CONTRACT**

Writer shall be deemed to have approved of said settlement or compromise.

15. NOTICES. Any written notices which Publisher shall desire to give to Writer hereunder, and all statements, royalties and other payments which shall be due to Writer hereunder, shall be addressed to Writer at the address set forth at the beginning of this agreement until Writer shall give Publisher written notice of a new address. All notices which Writer shall desire to give to Publisher hereunder shall be addressed to Publisher at the address set forth at the beginning of this agreement until Publisher shall give Writer written notice of a new address, and a courtesy copy of all such notices shall also be given to [Publisher Attorney's Name and Address]. All such notices shall either be served by hand (to an officer of Publisher if Publisher shall be the addressee) or by registered or certified mail, postage prepaid, or by telegraph, charges prepaid, addressed as aforesaid. The date of making personal service or of mailing or of depositing in a telegraph office, whichever shall be first, shall be deemed the date of service.

16. ENTIRE AGREEMENT. This agreement supersedes any and all prior negotiations, understandings and agreements between the parties hereto with respect to the subject matter hereof. Each of the

**ANALYSIS**

| CONTRACT | ANALYSIS |
| --- | --- |
| parties acknowledges and agrees that neither party has made any representations or promises in connection with this agreement or the subject matter hereof not contained herein. | |
| 17. MODIFICATION, WAIVER, INVALIDITY, AND CONTROLLING LAW. This agreement may not be cancelled, altered, modified, amended or waived, in whole or in part, in any way, except by an instrument in writing signed by the party sought to be bound. The waiver by either party of any breach of this agreement in any one or more instances shall in no way be construed as a waiver of any subsequent breach of this agreement (whether or not of a similar nature). If any part of this agreement shall be held to be void, invalid or unenforceable, it shall not affect the validity of the balance of this agreement. This agreement shall be deemed to have been made in the State of New York and its validity, construction and effect shall be governed by the laws of the State of New York applicable to agreements wholly performed therein. This agreement shall not be binding upon Publisher until signed by Writer and countersigned by a duly authorized officer of Publisher. | |
| 18. ASSIGNMENT. Publisher shall have the right to assign this agreement or any of its rights hereunder to any party which is or shall | 18. The publisher has the unlimited right to assign this contract to any party which may purchase all (or a substantial portion) of the owner- |

## CONTRACT

**be a subsidiary, affiliate or parent or to any party which shall acquire all or a substantial portion of Publisher's stock or assets.**

**19. DEFINITIONS. For the purposes of this agreement, "party" means and refers to any individual, corporation, partnership, association or any other organized group of persons or the legal successors or representatives of the foregoing. Whenever the expression "the term of this agreement" or words of similar connotation are used herein, they shall be deemed to mean and refer to the initial term of this agreement and any and all renewals, extensions, substitutions or replacements of this agreement, whether expressly indicated or otherwise.**

**20. SUSPENSION AND TERMINATION. If Writer shall fail, refuse or be unable to submit to Publisher two songs a month or shall otherwise fail, refuse or be unable to perform his material obligations hereunder, Publisher shall have the right, in addition to all of its other rights and remedies of law or in equity, to suspend the term of this agreement and its obligations hereunder by written notice to Writer, or, in the event such failure, refusal or inability shall continue for longer than six (6) months, to terminate this agreement by written notice to Writer. Any such suspension shall continue for the duration of any such failure, refusal or**

## ANALYSIS

ship of the publisher. This provision favors the writer by requiring the purchasing party to obtain, at least, a substantial portion of the publisher's business. This may give some assurance to the writer that the purchasing party is at least comparable in size to the publisher and has the wherewithal to succeed in its obligations to exploit the writer's copyrights.

**CONTRACT**

inability, and, unless Publisher notifies Writer to the contrary in writing, the then current term hereof shall be automatically extended by the number of days which shall equal the total number of days of suspension. During any such suspension Writer shall not render services as a songwriter and/or composer to any other party or assign, license or convey any musical composition to any other party.

21. HEADING. The heading of clauses or other divisions hereof are inserted only for the purposes of convenient reference. Such headings shall not be deemed to govern, limit, modify or in any other manner affect the scope, meaning or intent of the provisions of this agreement or any part thereof, nor shall they otherwise be given any legal effect.

22. CO-OWNERSHIP AND ADMINISTRATION. Notwithstanding any provision to the contrary herein contained, all Compositions shall be equally owned by Publisher and by Writer's designee, and shall be exclusively administered by Publisher, all in accordance with the terms and provisions of the Co-publishing Agreement annexed hereto as Exhibit "A".

ADDITIONAL CLAUSES

23. OTHER ARRANGEMENTS. Writer has entered or is entering

**ANALYSIS**

22. This paragraph further acknowledges that, pursuant to the co-publishing and administration agreement between the parties, the artist/songwriter's publishing company shall own an interest in the compositions.

23. This clause notes that the publisher/writer arrangement is part of an

**CONTRACT**

**into a recording contract with Publisher's production/record company affiliate. Notwithstanding any provision to the contrary herein contained, it is the intent of the parties hereto that the term of this agreement be coterminous with the term of said recording contract or of any successor or replacement agreement. Accordingly in the event said record company affiliate or its assignee fails to exercise any renewal option with respect to the recording contract or the successor or replacement agreement, Publisher shall not have the right to exercise any renewal option hereunder; further, any extension, renewal, suspension or termination of the recording contract or of the successor or replacement agreement by said record company affiliated or its assignee shall automatically and without further notice extend, renew, suspend or terminate this agreement in like manner.**

**24. RECOUPMENT. It is understood and acknowledged that any and all charges or advances against royalties under this agreement which are not recouped by Publisher may be recouped by Publisher's record company affiliate or its assignee from any and all royalties earned by Writer under the aforementioned recording contract or its successor or replacement agreement, and that any and all charges or advances against royalties under said recording contract or its successor or replacement**

**ANALYSIS**

Across the Board Deal, and as such, the Recording and Exclusive Songwriters Agreements are coterminous.

**CONTRACT** | **ANALYSIS**

agreement which are not recouped by said record company or its assignee may be recouped by Publisher from any and all royalties earned by Writer hereunder.

25. INDUCEMENT. Writer acknowledges that this agreement with Publisher is further consideration for Publisher's record company affiliate to enter into the recording contract hereinabove referred to, and that Writer is entering into this agreement to induce said record company affiliate to enter into said recording contract.

IN WITNESS WHEREOF, the parties hereto have executed this agreement as of the day and year first above written.

WRITER PUBLISHER

By:____________________

[Name of Publisher]
individually and as
Administrator for [Songwriter/
Artist Name] Publishing
Designee

# 10

# Co-Publishing and Administration Contract

## *Breakdown of Co-Publisher/Publisher Agreement*

**CONTRACT**

**Co-Publishing and Administration Agreement**

**THIS AGREEMENT made this _____ day of _________, by and between [Name of Production Co.'s Publishing Company] with offices located at [address of Publishing Company], (hereinafter referred to as "Company") and [Name and address of Songwriter/Artist] and/or his publishing designee (hereinafter referred to as "Participants").**

**WITNESSETH**

**WHEREAS, it is the intention of Company and Participants that they shall jointly own Participant's**

**ANALYSIS**

**Analysis of Co-Publishing and Administration Agreement**

The across the board deal arrangement for signing artists and songwriters became popular during the mid-1970s. Near the end of that decade, courts determined that the multiple contracts that provide the basis of this type of relationship could be voided unless the production company would allow the artist/songwriter to retain at least a 50% interest in the ownership of their copyrights. This Co-Publishing agreement, is a reflection of the effect of that rule.

It is an agreement between the production company's publishing

**CONTRACT**

**portion of the musical compositions (hereinafter referred to as "Composition" and collectively referred to as "Compositions") acquired by Company pursuant to Company's Exclusive Songwriter's Agreement of even date herewith with [Songwriter/Artist name] (hereinafter Songwriter's Agreement"), so that the entire universe-wide right, title and interest including the copyright, the right of copyright and any and all renewal rights, in and to Participants portion of the Compositions shall be owned by Company and by Participants in the percentages described below:**

**PERCENTAGES:**
**Company—50%**
**Participants—50%**

**WHEREAS, the Compositions shall be registered for copyright in the names of Company and Participants in the Copyright Office of the United States of America.**

**WHEREAS, Company and/or its affiliates [Production & Management Companies Names], have entered into a Management Agreement and Exclusive Recording and Songwriter's Agreement with [Songwriter/Artist name] (hereinafter Recording Agreement) of even date and it is hereby the intention of the parties that this agreement, the Management, Songwriter's and Recording Agreements be coterminous.**

**ANALYSIS**

company (referred to "Company") and the songwriter's publishing company (referred to as "Participant").

The contract's preamble describes and states that the Company and Participant shall share in the ownership of the copyrights owned hereunder on a 50%/50% basis.

## CONTRACT

**NOW THEREFORE, for good and valuable consideration the receipt of which is hereby acknowledged by each party hereto, it is agreed as follows:**

**1. Company and Participants shall jointly own Participant's portion of the Compositions conveyed pursuant to the Exclusive Songwriter's Agreement between Company and [name of Songwriter/Artist] dated ________, in the shares described above so that all the worldwide right, title and interest, including the copyrights, the right to copyright and any renewal rights therein and thereto shall be owned 50%—Company and 50% Participant. The phrase, "Participant's portion of the composition(s)," as used herein, shall be equivalent to Participant's pro rata percentage of songwriters contribution to the compositions.**

**2. The Compositions shall be registered for copyright by Company in the names of Company and Participants in the office of the Register of Copyrights of the United States of America. If any Composition has heretofore been registered for copyright in the name of Participants, Participants shall simultaneously herewith deliver to Company an assignment of the appropriate interest therein, in form acceptable to Company.**

**3. Participants hereby assign,**

## ANALYSIS

1. The "Participant's portion" of the composition relates only to the percentage of the copyright owned by the songwriter/artist should the songwriter/artist collaborate with another writer. If the songwriter/artist writes only 50% of the song, the Participant's portion of ownership of the composition shall only be 50% which, according to this contract, will be equally shared by the Participant and the Company.

2. The Company will be joint owner of the Participant's portion of the copyright. All the compositions acquired pursuant to the related exclusive songwriter's agreement shall be registered with the U.S. Copyright Office in the name of the Company and Participant.

3. The Participant agrees to grant to

| CONTRACT | ANALYSIS |
|---|---|
| transfer and grant to Company, its successors and assigns, licensees and subpublishers, the rights and responsibilities set forth below in and to the Compositions: | the Company a number of important rights, such as: |
| (a) The exclusive right to manage and administer throughout the Licensed Territory, all rights of every kind, nature and description in and to the Compositions, together with the right to manage and administer all copyrights and renewals or extensions thereof. | (a) the right to manage and administer Participant's interest in the copyrights throughout the territory; |
| (b) Participants hereby appoint Company as its sole exclusive agent throughout the Licensed Territory, for the purpose of collecting all income from sales and uses of the Compositions. Participants grant to Company the right to collect, on Participants' behalf, all gross income received heretofore unpaid, and now payable and all income which becomes payable during the term of this Agreement, from the date of original copyrights to the Compositions to be the effective date hereof and from all sales and uses of the Compositions, subject to accountings hereunder. | (b) the right to collect income from the exploitation of the compositions; |
| (c) The exclusive right to issue all licenses with respect to mechanical and electrical reproduction of the Compositions throughout the Licensed Territory on phonograph records, compact discs, prerecorded tapes, piano rolls and transcriptions, or by any other method | (c) the exclusive right to execute and issue all licenses with respect to mechanical reproduction of the compositions; |

**CONTRACT**

**now known and hereafter devised for sound reproduction and the licensing of the Compositions for such purposes throughout the Licensed Territory upon terms within the sole discretion of Company.**

**(d) The exclusive right to exploit and have others to perform through sound recordings of compositions for profit or otherwise by means of public performance, radio broadcast or any other means of media now known or hereafter conceived or developed throughout the universe.**

**(e) The exclusive right to grant licenses for the recording of the Compositions in and with motion pictures and television productions produced throughout the Licensed Territory, or making copies of the recordings thereof, and importing such copies into all countries of the world.**

**(f) The exclusive right to print, publish and sell printed music throughout the Licensed Territory in the form of sheet music, arrangements, song books, albums, portfolios or educational works and to authorize others to exercise said right. In connection with the foregoing and without any compensation other than as specified herein, Participants grant to Company the non-exclusive right to use and publish and to permit others to use and publish the names of any and all authors and/or writers of the Compo-**

**ANALYSIS**

(d) the right to exploit performances of the compositions by means of radio, television, internet or other media;

(e) the right to license the compositions for synchronization with motion pictures, television and other productions;

(f) the right to license and publish the compositions in printed music form;

**CONTRACT**

**sitions, (including any other professional name heretofore or hereafter adopted by such authors and/or writers), likenesses of, voice and sound effects and biographical material, or any reproduction or simulation thereof and titles of the Compositions. Company shall not use any artwork, photographs, likenesses of or biographical material relating to said individuals unless same have been approved by Participants or submitted to Company by Participants.**

**(g) The right to substitute a new title or titles for the Compositions and to make any change, arrangement, parody, adaptation, translation, or dramatization of the Composition, in whole or in part, and in connection with any other musical, literary or dramatic material as Company may deem expedient or desirable.**

**4. The term of this agreement shall commence upon the date hereof and shall continue for the term of the Recording Agreement, (a copy of the pertinent part**

**ANALYSIS**

(g) the right to substitute new titles or change or adapt the lyrics of the compositions;

While the Company is granted broad powers under this agreement, the attorney for the Participant may attempt to negotiate certain limits on the company's discretion to administer the compositions. It's possible that some forms of exploitation of the compositions may not appeal to the Participant, such as the use of a composition in a political commercial or objectionable movie or television program. The Participant may also object to the revision of a composition's lyrics. Under the terms of this agreement, the Participant is granting the Company the sole right and discretion to make these decisions, which could come back to haunt the Participant/Songwriter/Artist.

4. As a result of this contract being part of an "Across The Board Deal", it is coterminous with the Management, Exclusive Songwriters and Recording Agreements, which means

| CONTRACT | ANALYSIS |
|---|---|
| thereof are hereby attached hereto and incorporated herein and marked as attachment "A"), as same may be renewed or extended from time to time. Accordingly, each extension or renewal of the term of the Recording Agreement shall automatically extend or renew the term hereof for the same period. The phrase "the term hereof" or "the term of this agreement" as used in this agreement, shall refer to the initial and any extension or renewal terms hereof in accordance with the foregoing. Notwithstanding anything to the contrary herein, in the event either the Management, Co-Publishing or Songwriters Agreement are terminated for any reason prior to the end of that term of the recording agreement, all of the agreements between the parties shall terminate at that time. | that if one of these agreements end, they are all terminated. |
| 5. Company shall pay directly to Participants his publisher share and to the composition's writers their shares of the net income share due Participants and the composition's writers actually received and derived by company from the Compositions. "Net Income", as used herein, shall mean the gross receipts derived by Company from the Compositions less the following:<br><br>(a) Collection or other fees customarily and actually charged by any collection agent;<br><br>(b) Administration Fees | 5. The Participant shall receive its fifty percent (50%) publisher's share after all writers first receive their shares of net income. As you know in business in general the net income is defined as gross receipts less expenses. In the Publishing business that would include collection fees, administration charges charged by a third party, actual out of pocket administration or exploitation expenses such as mailings, copies, demo recordings, lead sheet transcribing, and attorneys fees directly related to a defense of claims regarding the interests granted hereunder. |

| CONTRACT | ANALYSIS |
|---|---|
| charged by any Third Party Administrator; | |
| (c) Actual, out-of-pocket administrative and exploitation expenses of Company with respect to the Composition for registration fee, advertising and promotion expenses directly related to the Compositions, the costs of transcribing for lead sheets, and the costs of producing demonstration records; | |
| (d) Attorneys' fees directly related to the defense of claims respecting the Compositions, if any, actually paid by Company; | |
| 6. The performing rights in the Compositions in the percentage as listed above, to the extent permitted by law, shall be assigned to and licensed by BMI or ASCAP as the case may be, which shall be and hereby is authorized to collect and receive all monies earned from the public performance of the Compositions and to pay directly to Company and Participants their share of one-hundred percent (100%) of the amount allocated by said performance rights society as the publisher's share of public performance fees. | 6. The performance rights organizations (ASCAP, BMI and SESAC) which license performing rights are authorized under this contract to pay royalties due the parties directly to the Company and Participant. In other words, the company does not have to account to the Participant for the share of the performance rights royalties because they are paid directly to each party. |
| 7. All mechanical royalties for the Compositions shall be collectible by such collection agent as may be designated by Company, provided however, that Company, may issue the mechanical licenses directly to said record company | 7. All mechanical royalties are collected directly by the Company, which accounts to and pays the Participant according to the accounting provision paragraph 8 hereunder which requires semi-annual statements within 90 days of the semi- |

**CONTRACT**

**and collect mechanical royalties directly therefrom in which case there shall be no collection fee as referred to Paragraph 5 hereinabove.**

**8. (a) Company shall render to Participants statements showing the amount of royalties payable hereunder for the semi-annual periods ending June 30th and December 31st, respectively, accompanied by payment of any royalties shown to be due in such statements within 90 days of the end of said semi-annual periods.**

**(b) At any time within one (1) year after any royalty statement is rendered to Participants hereunder, Participants shall have the right to give Company written notice of its intention to examine Company's books and records with respect to such statement. Such examination shall be commenced within six (6) months after the date of such notice, at Participants' sole cost and expense, by any certified public accountant or attorney designated by Participants, provided he is not then engaged in an outstanding examination of Company's books and records on behalf of a person other than Participants. Such examination shall be made during Company's usual business hours at the place where Company maintains the books and records which relate to Participants and which are necessary to verify the accuracy of the statement or state-**

**ANALYSIS**

annual periods ending June 30 and December 31 of each year.

8. This provision not only deals with the requirements for accounting to the Participant, but also indicates the Participant's right to audit or review the company's accounting. The Participant's right to audit is outlined in this paragraph and is limited to a prescribed period of one (1) year after receipt of the accounting statement. In my opinion, this provision is arguably too detail oriented, indicating who may audit (CPA/and/or Attorney not involved in current audit of books), when the audit may occur, (during regular hours, only once a year) and why, (to determine accuracy) which, if not challenged by an action by Participant within two (2) years, shall be deemed final and conclusive. This provision is pretty restrictive and as attorney for the Participant I would try to negotiate a less restrictive audit provision giving the Participant greater flexibility in auditing the Company's books.

**CONTRACT** | **ANALYSIS**

ments specified in Participants' notice to Company and Participants' right to inspect Company's books and records shall be only as set forth in this subparagraph and Company shall have no obligation to produce such books and records more than once with respect to each statement rendered to Participants. Unless notice shall have been given to Company as provided in this sub-paragraph, each royalty statement rendered to Participants shall be final, conclusive and binding upon Participants and shall constitute an account stated. Participants shall be foreclosed from maintaining any action, claim or proceeding against Company in any forum or tribunal with respect to any statement or accounting rendered hereunder unless a court of competent jurisdiction within two (2) years after the due date of such statement or accounting.

(c) Participants acknowledge that Company's books and records contain confidential trade information. Neither Participants nor its representatives will communicate with others or use on behalf of any other person any facts or information obtained as a result of such examination of Company's books and records.

9. Each party hereto shall give the other the equal benefits of any warranties or representations

| CONTRACT | ANALYSIS |
|---|---|
| which it obtains or shall obtain under any agreements affecting the Compositions. | |
| 10. Upon written request by Company, Participants shall promptly deliver to Company (a) typed lyric sheets of the Compositions and (b) copies of photographs, likenesses, and biographical material of the writer or writers of the Compositions. | |
| 11. Company shall have the sole right to prosecute, defend, settle and compromise all suits, claims and actions respecting the Compositions, and generally to do and perform all things necessary concerning the same and the copyrights therein, to prevent and restrain the infringement of copyrights or other rights with respect to the Compositions. In the event of the recovery of Company of any monies, less an amount equal to the expense of obtaining said monies, including counsel fees shall be deemed additional gross receipts hereunder. Company will credit Participants' account hereunder with Participants' applicable share of such monies as set forth in Paragraph 5 hereof, and will pay Participants, within thirty (30) days after receipt of such monies by Company, the net credit balance of Participants' account, if any Company will not settle any claim respecting the Compositions without Participants' consent, which consent shall not be unreasonably withheld. | 11. The Company shall also have the sole right to proceed in any action with respect to the Composition (i.e., claim for copyright infringement by a party who samples a composition subject to this agreement) and, if it is successful, will split the proceeds equally with Participant, less any expenses. |

**CONTRACT**

**12. The rights of the parties hereto in and to the Compositions shall extend for the term of the copyright of the Compositions and of any derivative copyrights therein in the United States of America throughout the rest of the world and for the terms of any renewals or extensions thereof in the United States of America and throughout the rest of the world.**

**13. Participants hereby warrant and represent that they are under no disability, restriction, or prohibition with respect to their right to enter into this agreement and to grant to Company all of the rights granted herein, and that the exercise by Company of any and all of the rights granted to Company in this agreement will not violate or infringe upon any common law or statutory rights of any person, firm or corporation, including, without limitation, contractual rights, copyrights and rights of privacy. The rights granted herein are free and clear of any claims, demands, liens or encumbrances. Participants agree to and do hereby indemnify, save and hold Company, it assigns, licensees, and its and their directors, officers, shareholders, agents and employees harmless from any and all liabilities, claims, demands, loss and damage (including attorneys' fees, and court costs) arising out of or connected with any claim by a third party which is inconsistent with any of the warranties, representations, covenants, or**

**ANALYSIS**

12. A publishing administration contract differs from a co-publishing agreement in an important aspect. The parties' rights to the composition (most importantly, the right of the company to administer and own 50% of Participant's portion of the Copyright) extend for the full term of the copyright and any renewals or extensions. If this deal were a publishing administration contract the company would not have any ownership in the copyrights of the Participants, but would only have the exclusive right to administer the copyrights for a fixed period of time usually for a set percentage (10%-25%) of the income generated during the term after which the rights to administration would revert back to the Participant. Therefore, in a publishing administration contract the Participant receives the dual benefit of retaining the right of ownership of the copyrights, while affiliating with a publisher, who, for a fee, uses its expertise to more fully exploit the participants catalog of copyrights.

## CONTRACT

agreements made by Participants herein and Participants agree to reimburse Company, on demand, for any payment made by Company at any time after the date hereof with respect to any liability or claim to which the foregoing indemnity applies. Pending the determination of any such claim, Company may withhold payment of royalties or other monies hereunder, provided that all amounts so withheld are reasonably related to the amount of said claim and the estimated attorney's fees in connection therewith, and provided further that Participants shall have the right to post a bond in an amount reasonably satisfactory to Company by a bonding Company reasonably satisfactory to Company, in which event Company shall not withhold payments as aforesaid.

14. In the event that Participants receive a bona fide offer from a third party (the "Third Party Offer") to purchase all or any portion of Participants interest in a composition or of any of them and Participants desire to sell such interest, Participants agree to first offer in writing to sell such interest to Company (the "First Offer") upon all the terms and conditions set forth in the Third Party Offer. Such First Offer shall specify all of the terms and conditions of the Third Party Offer and in the event Company does not, within thirty (30) days after receipt by Company of the First Offer, accept the First Of-

## ANALYSIS

14. This provision, a right of first refusal clause, allows the company to match any third party offer made to the Participant for its ownership share of a particular copyright or the entire catalog. This is accomplished by imposing certain time limitations and restrictions on the company's right to match a third party offer which, as a result, provides the company the opportunity to maintain an ownership interest in copyrights it may have created value in through its exploitation efforts. Of course the Participant's attorney may ask that a similar provision be inserted in favor of the Participant should the company desire to sell its interests.

**CONTRACT** | **ANALYSIS**

fer, then Participants shall have the right to accept the Third Party Offer; provided, however, that the sale to such third party shall be consummated within one hundred twenty (120) days after receipt of the First Offer by Company and, provided further, that the sale to such third party shall be upon all of the terms and conditions contained in the First Offer. If such sale is not consummated, Participants shall not sell all or any portion of its interest in the Composition or any of them without first offering to sell such interest to Company as hereinbefore set forth.

15. Any notice, consent, approval, demand, or other communication to be given or sent to the other party hereunder must be in writing and shall be deemed to have been duly given or sent if delivered personally or if sent by registered mail to the address first hereinabove stated or to such other address as either party may send to the other party by like notice. Except as otherwise herein stated, the date of mailing or of actual personal delivery of any such communication shall be deemed the date upon which such communication was given or sent.

16. This Agreement shall not be deemed to give any right or remedy to third party whatsoever unless said right or remedy is specifically granted to such third party by the terms hereof.

| **CONTRACT** | **ANALYSIS** |
|---|---|
| **17. The parties hereto shall execute any further documents including, without limitation, assignments of copyrights, and do all acts necessary to fully effectuate the terms and provisions of this agreement. Participants hereby irrevocably appoint Company or any of its officers as its true and lawful attorney-in-fact to make, sign, execute, acknowledge, and deliver in its name any and all instruments which Company may deem desirable to vest in Company, its successors, assigns, and licenses any or all of the rights herein granted to Company.** | 17. The Participant appoints the Company as its attorney-in-fact, enabling the company to execute licenses, copyright forms, transfers, and assignments in the Participant's name should the Participant not be available to authorize such actions. This assures the Company that it may vest the rights granted hereunder if the Participant inadvertently fails to do so. |
| **18. Company may enter into subpublishing agreements with, or assign, or license any of its rights hereunder to, one or more other persons, firms, or corporations for any one or more countries of the world. In the event Company enters into a subpublishing or administration agreement for any country of the world with a company affiliated with or otherwise related to Company, such agreement shall be deemed to have been made with an independent third party. Participants acknowledge that Company has the right to administer and publish compositions other than the Compositions.** | 18. The Company also has the right to enter into sub-publishing contracts with other companies. In this agreement, it is also specified that the Company may enter into a contract with an affiliate for this purpose. If so the affiliate will be deemed an independent third party to the Company. This may allow the Company to, in essence, double dip, by allowing its foreign affiliate to take a fee off the top before the Company is required to split the balance with Participant. The Participant's attorney may desire to have this fee lowered or eliminated entirely to prevent the double dipping aspects of such a transaction. |
| **19. Company shall have the right to assign, sell or license this Agreement in whole or in part at any time during the term hereof to any person, firm or corporation, including but not limited to any of** | 19. You'll see here that the company also has the right, without restrictions, to assign this contract. The Participant could consider this unrestricted right a potential problem and may seek to have it limited. You see, |

**CONTRACT**

**Company's affiliates or subsidiaries. However, no such assignment, sale or license shall relieve Company of its obligations hereunder without the express written consent of participants.**

**20. This Agreement sets forth the entire understanding between the parties, and cannot be changed, modified, or cancelled except by an instrument signed by the party sought to be bound.**

**21. It is understood and acknowledged that any and all charges or advances against royalties made by Company to Participant under this and/or any other agreement between the parties which are not recouped by Company may be recouped by Company's production company affiliate or its assignee from any and all royalties earned by Participant under the aforementioned recording agreement or its successor or replacement agreement and that any and all charges or advances against royalties under said recording agreement or its successor or replacement agreement which are not recouped by said production company or its assignee may be recouped by Company from any and all royalties earned by Participant hereunder.**

**This Agreement shall be governed by and construed under the laws of the State of New York ap-**

**ANALYSIS**

in many instances, a Participant may execute this type of contract because of a special relationship with specific personnel of the Company and therefore will not want the Company to assign the agreement to another Company without its prior consent.

21. This last paragraph allows the cross-collateralization of publishing royalties against all advances from the Company or any of its affiliates. The company may insist on its inclusion because of the sizable up front investment its production company affiliate has made in recording the songwriter/artist. As I indicated earlier, since significant costs of videos and independent promotion are routinely made recoupable from record royalties, the only effective stream of earnings for the songwriter/artist may be the copyright earnings subject to this agreement. I strongly recommend resisting any attempt to have this important stream of earnings used to offset the costs of any other agreement executed by the artist/songwriter.

**CONTRACT**

**ANALYSIS**

**plicable to agreements wholly performed therein.**

**IN WITNESS WHEREOF, the parties have executed this Agreement the day and year above set forth.**

**"PARTICIPANT"**

______________________________

**"COMPANY"**

______________________________

11

# Statement and Analysis of Copyright Earnings

## *How the Copyright Money Flows*

The following statement and analysis of copyright earnings will help you see the flow of monies through the preceding songwriters and co-publishing and administration agreements to the songwriter and his or her production company's publishing affiliate.

As I indicated earlier, the copyright is the most important asset in the music business, particularly to the artist-songwriter, because if his or her recording agreement is properly negotiated, the copyright earnings should not be cross-collateralized with the recording agreement or be used to help recoup the myriad costs associated with the recording process. Therefore, while an artist-songwriter may not realize artist royalties for his or her recording services due to the high costs associated with producing and marketing the records, that same artist-songwriter may realize income from copyright earnings from the first sale or air play of his or her records. In today's music business, this may make the difference in the artist surviving from one record project to the next.

The following statement of copyright earnings is for a fictitious single composition entitled "Can't Get Enough" and it tracks the earnings generated from the exploitation of the mechanical, performance, derivative, and synchronization rights of the song. Keep in mind that the earnings presented here are for only one song. Suppose the artist-songwriter had written eight to ten other songs contained on the CD which "Can't Get Enough" appeared on. If so, you could multiply these earnings by eight to ten times and, I guarantee you, you'll see why the copyright is so valuable. And remember, if "Can't Get Enough" is sampled on another record ten years from now or recorded by another artist during that time, the money just keeps rolling in.

I recently read an article about William Devaughn, the artist-songwriter who wrote one hit in the 1970s, entitled "Be Thankful for What You've Got." You might remember the hook of that song: "Diamond in the back, sun roof top, diggin' in the scene with a gangster lean . . ." He says that while it was his only hit, with the multiple uses, continued air play, and the sampling of the song since it was released, he's earned over $1 million from that song alone over the years. As I always say, whenever the music is played, somebody gets paid!

Usually the songwriter-author enters into a songwriter agreement with a publisher, whose job it is to exploit the song. In the case of a typical songwriter agreement, the songwriter ("author") grants the entire copyright to the publisher for a certain period of years or for the term of the copyright. In this example, the publisher, in exchange for 50% of the earnings derived from the copyrighted works, agrees to use its best efforts to protect, exploit, collect income, and account for such income to the author. (In some cases, the publisher may receive an additional 10 to 15% as an administration fee.) The publisher may attempt to sign the songwriter to a long-term exclusive songwriter agreement, as is the case in our example. In this instance, the songwriter is required to grant to the publisher every copyright he or she creates during the term of the agreement.

This following statement and analysis cover the four primary income-generating rights of the copyright's "bundle of rights" and their resulting income stream. The first income stream is from the exploitation of the performance right.

---

### 1.) PERFORMANCE RIGHT

Publisher and songwriters affiliate with either ASCAP, BMI, or SESAC to license copyrights for performance. If ASCAP, BMI, or SESAC determine that the composition earned a total of $10,000 in royalties and pays 50% directly to the publisher and 50% directly to the songwriter.

**Earnings:**

$10,000 As determined by performance rights organization's royalty calculation

**ASCAP/BMI/SESAC**

Pays $10,000.00 Royalties Directly to:

| Publisher (50%) | Songwriter (50%) |
|---|---|
| $5,000 | $5,000 |

---

As I explained in the section on copyright principles, this right is usually exploited by one of the Big Three performance rights organizations, BMI, ASCAP, or SESAC, pursuant to an affiliation agreement between the performance rights organization, the publisher, and the songwriter. Under the terms of these agreements, the monies calculated to be earned from the song by the performance rights organization are divided equally and paid directly to the publisher and the songwriter from the performance rights organization. In this example, that amount is $10,000, with the publisher being paid $5,000 and the songwriter $5,000. Keep in mind that if there are multiple publishers or songwriters for a particular composition, these payments must be pro-rated according to each party's interest in the composition.

The second stream of income from the copyright is derived from the exploitation of the mechanical right.

## 2.) MECHANICAL RIGHT

Publisher issues mechanical license to Record Company requiring mechanical royalty 7.55¢ Minimum Statutory Rate (M.S.R) or 5.66¢ (3/4s of M.S.R.) per mechanical reproduction.

### Earnings:

200,000 CDs
100,000 Cassettes
100,000 Cassette Singles

400,000 Total Units containing mechanical reproductions of the composition entitled: "Can't Get Enough"
x 7.55¢ Mechanical royalty per unit

$30,200 Total mechanical royalties owed to publisher by record company

### Record Company—Pays

Total Mechanical
Royalties of $30,200 directly to publisher

### Publisher—Keeps 50%

Total Mechanical Royalties ($15,100)
Pays 50% ($15,100) to

### Songwriter

Pursuant to Songwriter's Agreement

The mechanical right is exploited through the use of a mechanical license issued by the copyright owner (usually the publisher of the composition) to the record company who manufactures and distributes the recording. Usually, as a result of the application of the controlled composition clause of the exclusive recording artist agreement, the record company pays only three-quarters (¾) of the minimum statutory mechanical royalty rate of 7.55¢ or 5.66¢ per mechanical reproduction of the composition. However, in this example, we will assume that the record company pays the full minimum statutory mechanical royalty rate of 7.55¢ per mechanical reproduction. "Can't Get Enough" sold a total of 400,000 units containing the copyrighted work, so a total of $30,200 is payable from the record company to the publisher. You may recall that under the terms of the exclusive songwriter contract, the publisher is allowed to collect the entire amount of mechanical royalties due from the record company. The publisher, in turn, is also required to pay the songwriter, on a semiannual basis, 50% of the mechanical royalties collected. In my example, the publisher is entitled to collect $30,200 from the record company and must pay the songwriter 50% of the monies ($15,100) when it submits its account to the songwriter. It's important to note that as the publisher only has to account to the songwriter on a six-month basis, it is allowed to earn extra income by holding the songwriter's royalties until the six-month payout. This is because the U.S. Copyright Act requires manufacturers and distributors to pay mechanical royalties to the copyright owners on a quarterly basis. Consequently, the publisher, who collects the mechanical royalties from the record company every three months, is allowed to earn interest on the money it owes the songwriter until it is required to pay the songwriter after six months.

The derivative right is the third income generating source.

---

**3.) Derivative Right**

Movie Company makes movie based on lyrics of the copyrighted composition

**Earnings:**

Flat Buyout of $25,000

**Movie Company—Pays**

Entire $25,000 to Publisher

**Publisher—Keeps**

50% ($12,500)

Pays 50% ($12,500) to

**Songwriter**

Pursuant to Songwriter Agreement

---

Suppose a movie company makes a movie entitled *Can't Get Enough*, the theme and story of which are substantially similar to the lyrics of the composition. In order not to infringe on the copyright of the composition, the movie company must license the right to base the story on the lyrics of the composition for a one-time payment ($25,000, for example) to the publisher. Under the terms of the songwriter contract, the publisher would pay one-half of the sum, in this case $12,500, to the songwriter.

The synchronization right is the last source of income we'll consider in this example.

---

**4.) Synchronization Right**

Television movie uses master recording of "Can't Get Enough".

**Earnings:**

Flat buyout fee of $10,000:

**Movie Company—Pays**

Entire $10,000 to Publisher

**Publisher—Keeps**

50% ($5,000)

Pays 50% ($5,000) to

**Songwriter**

Pursuant to Songwriter Agreement

---

As covered in the copyright principles section, the synchronization right is the right to synchronize the copyright from one medium to another. In my example, the master recording of "Can't Get Enough" is incorporated in a made-for-television movie. The network pays a one-time flat buyout fee of $10,000 for this right. This amount is also paid directly to the publisher, who accounts for half (or $5,000) to the songwriter pursuant to the songwriter agreement.

With respect to the derivative right and synchronization right, keep in mind that, while in our example, a one-time flat buyout fee of all uses of the product (videocassettes, cable, overseas sales, etc.) was paid for these rights, it is possible to have it negotiated so that separate payments will be made for the various uses of the product. In other words, it is possible for the copyright owner to be paid one fee for the movie to run in theaters, and additional amounts for videocassettes, foreign runs, and other ancillary uses of the movie.

### Summary of Copyright Earnings of Copyright Entitled "Can't Get Enough"

| | *Total Earned* | *Publisher's Share* | *Songwriter's Share* |
|---|---|---|---|
| 1.) Performance Income | $10,000.00 | $5,000.00 | $5,000.00 |
| 2.) Mechanical Income | $30,200.00 | $15,100.00 | $15,100.00 |
| 3.) Derivative Income | $25,000.00 | $12,500.00 | $12,500.00 |
| 4.) Synchronization Income | $10,000.00 | $5,000.00 | $5,000.00 |
| TOTAL | $75,200.00 | $37,600.00 | $37,600.00 |

Looking at the bottom-line figures of this example should also help you realize the importance of the publisher's share of copyright income. That is why many artists and songwriters attempt to publish their own works, thereby keeping the publisher's share for themselves or co-publishing with a larger, more effective publishing company and splitting the publisher's share equally.

12

# Personal Management Contract

## *A Preview*

The personal management contract and the statement and analysis of management earnings, deal with the very important manager–artist relationship. Its place in this book has nothing to do with its level of importance. A manager's role in the development and guidance of an artist's career is crucial. A manager's job is to help the artist navigate his or her career through the uncharted, shark-ridden waters that the music business emulates at times. In these times it seems that a manager must be as multidimensional and multimedia savvy as possible. The ability for artists to cross over from the music business into television and movies is greater now than ever before. Just consider artists like Brandy, Whitney Houston, Queen Latifah, and Usher. These artists, like their predecessors, such as Elvis Presley, Glen Campbell, and Isaac Hayes, all started in music, but expanded the breadth of their exposure to include the broader mediums of television and movies. Managers have the responsibility of recommending the proper time, venue, and mediums to expose and exploit the many talents of artists—a big responsibility, particularly when you consider that the manager holds the fate of the artist's career in his or her hands.

While managing an artist's musical activities may be the genesis of the artist's career, a manager's outlook should be focused on building and maintaining a long, successful career for the artist. My dad always told me to "look with the long view," in other words, think about what you'll be doing twenty to thirty years from now. A perfect example of managing with a "long view" is displayed by the recent success of the Temptations. After not having a gold album in over ten years, their 1998 release of the LP Phoenix Rising has sold over 1,000,000 copies. Never mind that most record executives feel there is no large market for any artist over 34 years old. This group, started almost forty years ago, proved that with dedication to excellence and proper guidance, success can be achieved against the odds. Their manager, Shelly Berger, has managed them since the 1960s. While Shelly and I have had our disagreements over the years, I must admit that the promotional plan of having The Temptations perform at the 1998 Super Bowl, coupled with their successful television miniseries in November 1998, was a stroke of genius in exposing them to their old fans as well as developing new ones. Just think—forty years—now *that's* the long view.

As you review the terms of and comments to the sample personal management agreement and statement and analysis of the manager's earnings, bear in mind that due to the "across the board" aspect of the manager's relationship with the artist, the manager cannot earn a commission on recording or copyright earnings generated by the artist. As a result of the manager's contract, her or his sole source of income will be from the exploitation of the artist's other talents or income-generating opportunities resulting from the success of such talents. However, with the recent explosion of multimedia opportunities available to successful musical artists, the manager's, as well as the artist's potential for earning big bucks from the artist's career is greater than ever before.

CONTRACT

## PERSONAL MANAGEMENT AGREEMENT

**AGREEMENT made as of the day of _____________, by and between [Name and Address of Production Company's Management Company] (hereinafter sometimes referred to as "Manager") and [Individual Group Members Names and Addresses], jointly and individually and collectively professionally known as "[Group Name]" (hereinafter sometimes individually and collectively referred to as "Artist").**

**WHEREAS, Artist is desirous of engaging the services of Manager to act as Artist's personal advisor and counselor and to attend to certain business details in connection with Artist's professional career in the entertainment industry; and**

**WHEREAS, Manager is willing to become associated with Artist and act as the manager for Artist upon the terms and conditions hereinafter set forth;**

**WHEREAS, Manager, its record company and publishing company affiliates have entered into an Exclusive Recording, Co-Publishing and Songwriters Agreement, respectively, with Artist or Artist designees of even date and it is hereby the intention of the parties that the term hereof shall be coterminous with the term of the Exclusive Recording Agreement.**

ANALYSIS

## ANALYSIS OF PERSONAL MANAGEMENT AGREEMENT

This contract, as with most contracts in the music business, binds all the members of a group, both individually and collectively. If the contract terminates for one group member, it will still be binding for the other group members. In his book entitled "Truly Blessed", Teddy Pendergrass mentioned that when he first signed a recording agreement with Philadelphia International Records, each member of his group, The Bluenotes, was signed individually. When he decided to quit the group, Philadelphia International exercised its right to record him as a solo artist. While the company had the right to continue to record the other members of the remaining Bluenotes, upon the urging of Pendergrass, the company released them from this obligation.

As stated in the preamble of this contract, the role of a manager is to provide the services of a personal advisor and counsellor to the artist, attending to certain business details in connection with the artist's career. In many instances, artists look to managers to finance or bankroll their career endeavors. While this may be the case in some instances (as you will see in certain provisions of this contract), the manager is not a "bank" and is under no obligation to finance any of the artist's activities or pay personal bills for the artist while the artist is pursuing his or her career.

**CONTRACT**

**NOW, THEREFORE, in consideration of the foregoing and the mutual promises and covenants hereinafter contained, it is agreed as follows:**

**1. Artist hereby engages Manager as Artist's sole and exclusive personal manager in the entertainment industry throughout the world during the Term of this Agreement, and Manager hereby accepts such engagement subject to the terms and conditions set forth herein. The term of this Agreement shall commence as of the date hereof and shall continue for the term of the Recording Agreement (a copy of the pertinent part thereof are hereby attached hereto and incorporated herein and marked as "Attachment A"), as same may be renewed or extended from time to time. Accordingly, each extension or renewal of the term of the Recording Agreement shall automatically extend or renew the term hereof for the same period. The phrase "the term hereof" or "term of this agreement" as used in this agreement, shall refer to the initial and any extension of renewal of terms hereof in accord with the foregoing. Notwithstanding anything to the contrary herein, in the event either the Management, Co-Publishing or Songwriter's Agreements are terminated for any reason prior to the end of that term of the recording agreement, all of the agreements between the partes shall terminate at that time.**

**ANALYSIS**

1. When the artist engages a manager it is usually done on an exclusive basis. In other words, the artist has only one manager during the term of the contract. As will be discussed later in paragraph 5 of this agreement while the management relationship is exclusive to the artist, it is not exclusive to the manager, which means the manager is free to represent other artists during the term of the contract.

| **CONTRACT** | **ANALYSIS** |
| --- | --- |
| **2. Manager agrees, subject to Artist's availability and cooperation, to perform the following personal management services, at the request of Artist, in connection with Artist's activities in the entertainment industry:**<br><br>**(a) advise and counsel in the selection of any literary, artistic and musical material;**<br><br>**(b) advise and counsel in any and all matters pertaining to any public relations and advertising for Artist;**<br><br>**(c) advise and counsel with relation to the adoption of the proper format for presentation of Artist's talents and in the determination of proper style, mood and setting therefor;**<br><br>**(d) advise, counsel and direct in the selection of any artistic talent to work with Artist;**<br><br>**(e) advise and counsel with regard to general practices in the entertainment and amusement industries, and with respect to compensation and terms of contracts in such industries;**<br><br>**(f) advise and counsel concerning the selection of theatrical agencies and persons, firms and corporations to procure employment and engagements for Artist;**<br><br>**(g) negotiate any and all agreement(s) pertaining to Artist's ser-** | 2. Under the terms of this contract, the manager agrees to provide, at the request of the artist, advice and counsel in various areas. This includes the selection of material, matters relating to public relations, format and presentation of the artist's performance, and selection of artistic talent to work with the artist. The manager also advises as to general practices of the entertainment industry with respect to compensation and terms of contracts in the industry. In regards to the manager offering counsel to the artist in respect of compensation and terms of contracts it is important for the artist to insist upon the manager obtaining advice from a competent attorney as to these matters. As I indicated earlier, compensation and terms of contracts in this industry change so rapidly as a result of such dynamics as developing technology and business conditions (i.e., mergers, takeovers and bankruptcies) it is incumbent on managers to reach out to the attorney, whose job it is to keep abreast of these changes in order to best serve the interests of the artist. Please note that in paragraph 2(h) of the contract the manager is required to "use manager's reasonable efforts to endeavor to advance promising aspects of the artist's career." This is a great provision to have in the contract if you're the manager. The words "reasonable and promising" are very subjective terms and are open to broad interpretation. Who's supposed to determine what's reasonable and what's promising? This is an important question that's not (but should be) answered in this |

**CONTRACT**

**vices, but only to the extent permitted by law (Artist agreeing in any event to obtain Manager's prior written approval of each of same); and**

**(h) use Manager's reasonable efforts to endeavor to advance promising aspects of Artist's career.**

**ANALYSIS**

contract. Due to the "Across The Board" deal nature of the Production Company's agreements with the artist, the management contract is coterminous with the Exclusive Recording Artist Contract. Most managers argue that they need a two to three year initial term in order to develop a new artist's career to reach certain level of respectibility. With this in mind, the artist's attorney should insist that more definite standards be incorporated into the contract obligating the manager to achieve a certain level of performance in order to have the right to extend the term into the option years. Achievements such as obtaining a recording agreement for the artist within the first year or helping the artist achieve minimum gross earnings in excess of a certain figure (i.e, $200,000 per year) should be required in order for the manager to earn the right to continue to represent the artist during the option years.

**3. Artist agrees that Manager is not expected to, nor shall Manager procure or secure employment for Artist. Manager is not to perform any services which, standing alone, shall constitute Manager a talent agent, and Manager has not agreed or promised to perform such services except to the extent permitted by any applicable laws. Artist agrees to utilize proper talent or other employment agencies to obtain engagements and employment for Artist after first submitting the names thereof to Manager, and not to engage or retain any talent or**

3. Most management contracts clearly state that the manager is not a booking agent and is not obligated to obtain employment for the artist. In certain states, regulations exist which prohibit managers from performing any services which may cause them to be deemed a talent agent. The states of New York and California have strict laws regulating talent agencies whose job is to procure employment for the artist. If a manager procures employment for the artist violating those regulations, they may be severely penalized. In California, for instance, a manager who provides the services of

**CONTRACT**

**other employment agency of which Manager may disapprove. Artist further agrees to submit all offers of employment (and all leads or other communications related thereto) and all contracts of any kind to Manager for Manager's advice and counsel and, if and to the extent permitted by applicable laws, approval.**

**4. (a) If Artist is, in the sole discretion of Manager, not reasonably available to execute any employment agreement (or related or similar written instrument) not requiring Artist's exclusive services for in excess of seven (7) full days, Manager may, at Manager's sole election, execute such agreement (or instrument) as Artist's attorney-in-fact. Manager shall also be authorized, in Manager's discretion, on Artist's behalf, to approve and permit any and all publicity and advertising for Artist and to approve and permit the use of Artist's name, photograph, likeness, caricatures, voice and/or sound effects for the purposes of advertising and publicity and/or in the promotion of any and all products and services, and Artist shall not approve or permit any of the foregoing without Manager's approval thereof.**

**ANALYSIS**

a talent agency is acting in violation of the state's regulations. If this happens the artist may bring the manager before that state's labor commissioner who could terminate the management contract as well as order the manager to repay all commissions they may have earned during the term of the contract. Therefore, most managers take great pains to leave the procurement of employment to booking agencies licensed to perform this important function. The manager may, however, want the right to approve the booking agency and the terms of any agreement submitted to the artist before the artist's acceptance of such engagement.

4. I feel that this paragraph is one of the most important clauses in any management contract because it grants the manager a power of attorney to act on the artist's behalf in situations where the artist's signature may be needed. This power of attorney gives the manager the right to act on the artist's behalf. From my perspective as a lawyer and performer, I know this clause should be as narrowly limited as possible, only giving the manager the right to sign on the artist's behalf in special instances. In this contract, the manager is granted the power of attorney to sign contracts for performance engagements limited to seven (7) days or less. Any engagement less than seven days may be executed by the manager and will legally commit the artist to that engagement. However, a recording contract with a term of one year or a

**CONTRACT**

**(b) (i) Artist hereby irrevocably appoints Manager as Artist's true and lawful attorney to collect and receive for Artist all compensation or other income or payments intended for Artist, which portion is payable to Manager hereunder (and Manager may deduct therefrom and retain any monies due Manager hereunder and/or deduct from any portion of such compensation, income or payments and pay therefrom any monies due any third party for any reason), as well as endorse, sign, make, execute and deliver all checks, drafts, notes and bills of exchange that may be drawn in Artist's name which are payable with respect to Artist's services and Artist hereby gives Manager the full power, right and authority to do any or all of the foregoing as Manager shall, in Manager's sole discretion, deem advisable in as full and ample a manner as Artist could do if personally present and Artist hereby ratifies and confirms all that Manager shall do or cause to be done by reason thereof, except as may be otherwise expressly provided elsewhere in this Agreement.**

**(ii) Notwithstanding any provision to the contrary contained herein, Manager shall not execute any recording agreements, motion picture agreements or any other agreement which will require Artist to render services for one (1) year or more without obtaining Artist's prior consent.**

**ANALYSIS**

month long engagement in Vegas or Atlantic City cannot be signed on the artist's behalf by the manager. This contract also grants the manager the power to approve all publicity and use of the artist's name and likeness for the promotion of various aspects of the artist's career. This provision also grants the manager the power to collect and receive all compensation intended for the artist, giving the manager the right to endorse checks made payable to the artist as well as sign checks drawn on the artist's bank accounts. The manager may also deduct their commission from the funds received on behalf of the artist. Should the artist receive any gross compensation directly, the artist is deemed to be holding such funds in trust for the manager and within forty eight (48) hours of receipt the artist is required to transfer the funds to the manager. The artist also agrees to instruct any party from whom the artist expects to receive compensation, to pay the funds to the manager directly. The artist shouldn't be in favor of this type of provision unless he or she has a lot of faith and trust in the manager. While it is my preference for the artist to be the first one to receive any compensation, and subsequently pay the manager their commissions, I understand the manager's desire to be "kept in the loop" regarding the payment of commissionable income. If the manager is the first point of receipt of the artist's funds, as is the case here, the contract should also have a time and

**CONTRACT**

**(c) In the event any gross compensation (as hereinafter defined) which should have been paid to Manager pursuant to the terms of this Agreement is nonetheless received at any time by Artist or by any other person, firm or corporation or other entity(ies) of any kind or nature on Artist's behalf, including, without limitation, any agent and/or business manager, same shall be deemed to be held in trust for Manager, and Artist shall immediately require the source of such gross compensation to thereafter conform to the provisions of this Paragraph 4 and shall, within forty-eight (48) hours of receipt of such gross compensation, remit or cause the remittance of all such gross compensation to Manager from the first monies so received and prior to the payment of any other monies, and a photocopy of this Agreement shall (and hereby does) serve as an irrevocable letter of direction, authorizing and directing any and all other persons, firms and corporations or other entity(ies) to at all times so remit such gross compensation as provided above.**

**(d) Artist hereby warrants and agrees that any and all agreements entered into by, for or concerning Artist during the Term hereof (including any extensions and renewals thereof) shall provide for payment directly to Manager in accordance with the provisions of this Paragraph 4, and that Artist shall promptly execute and deliver to**

**ANALYSIS**

method by which the manager must account to and pay funds due to the artist. Similarly, if the artist is the first point of receipt of compensation, he or she should be contractually obligated to pay the manager's commission in a prompt and timely manner. The artist also acknowledges in this paragraph that the manager is not required to make any loans or advances. If the manager does loan or advance money to the artist, the artist agrees to repay the manager promptly.

As I mentioned earlier, while the manager's agreement is exclusive to the artist, who can have only one manager, it is not exclusive to the manager, who may represent other artists during the term of this contract. This, too is a provision the artist may try to have limited if the artist feels that the manager may represent an act similar to, and, as a result, in competition with the artist either at that time or in the future. The artist may therefore request a provision that limits the manager's right to represent other talents within the same category of music as the artist.

| CONTRACT | ANALYSIS |
|---|---|
| each other party to any such agreements already entered into an irrevocable letter of direction (in form acceptable to such party) effectuating the provisions of this Paragraph 4, and Artist further warrants and agrees that in the event any existing agreement is hereinafter amended, Artist shall cause such amendment, to include a provision for payment directly to Manager in the manner hereinabove set forth. | |
| (e) Artist acknowledges that Manager is not required to make any loans or advances to Artist, but in the event Manager does so, Artist agrees to repay Manager promptly and Manager is hereby irrevocably authorized to deduct the amount of such loans or advances from any sums which Manager may receive for Artist's account. | |
| 5. Artist understands that Manager may also represent other persons and performers and that Manager's services hereunder are not exclusive. Artist agrees that Manager shall not be required to devote Manager's entire time and attention to fulfilling Manager's obligations under this Agreement, and that Manager shall have the right to render services to other persons, firms and corporations either in the capacity which Manager is employed hereunder or otherwise. Artist warrants that Artist will actively pursue Artist's career in the | |

**CONTRACT**

**entertainment industry and will give due consideration to all advise and counsel proffered by Manager hereunder. Artist agrees at all times to be devoted to Artist's career and to do all things reasonably necessary to promote same.**

**6. (a) In full compensation for Manager's services hereunder, Artist shall pay to Manager, as and when received by Artist, or by Manager as provided herein, and prior to payment of any other party, twenty percent (20%) of the "gross compensation" ("Commission") of Artist, as hereinafter defined, received at any time on account of any and all activities in the entertainment and publishing industries except as specifically excluded from this Agreement. "Gross compensation", as used herein, shall mean the gross sums of money or other considerations (including, but not limited to, fees, salaries, earnings, royalties, residuals, advances, report and/or union fees, bonuses, proceeds of sales, leases or licenses, recording costs, gifts, shares of stock, partnership interests and amounts paid for packaged television, motion pictures and radio programs) directly or indirectly earned or received by Artist or Artist's heirs, successors and assigns, or earned, received or expended by anyone on Artist's behalf, from any professional activities of Artist (and/or derived from the use of Artist's experiences or talents and/or the results or proceeds thereof), whether as an actor,**

**ANALYSIS**

6. Industry observers have noticed over the years that it always seems that managers who commission on the artist's gross income inevitably end up in a conflict with the artist whose earnings are based on its net income. As the artist bears the enormous expense of maintaining its career, it usually ends up with only a fraction of what the manager makes. If the artist happens to be a group, the additional division of net income usually results in the act becoming jealous, resentful, and/or envious of the manager's rapid accumulation of wealth, while they're left with the daily task of working just to make ends meet, so to say. To avoid this eventuality, progressive managers may consider agreeing to other formulas regarding the commission process. In the seventies, it was reported that the late Benjamin Ashburn, then manager of the group, The Commodores (when Lionel Richie was a member), agreed to be made a partner with the group, in essence becoming a "sixth" member of the five-man group as far as being compensated for his services, thereby increasing his earnings along with and at the same rate as the group's members.

However in most instances a

**CONTRACT**

**writer, composer, author, lyricist, singer, musician, performer, artist, designer, cameraman, technician, director, producer, supervisor, executive, consultant or as owner in whole or in part of any properties, or as a stockholder or owner in whole or in part of any other kind of proprietary interest in a production, publishing or other firm or entity of any kind, and whether for the rendition of the Artist's services or from the sale or other disposition of literary, dramatic or musical property or package radio or television program, or any rights therein or thereto, or any use of Artist's name(s) (including, but not limited to [Group Name] or any other group or professional names individually or collectively used at any time by any member or members of Artist, alone or with others), likeness or talents for advertising purposes or otherwise, without any exclusion or deduction whatsoever, including all sums earned by Artist during the Term of this Agreement, and thereafter, under any employment or contract now in existence or entered into or negotiated for during the Term hereof, or under any extension, modification, addition or renewal of such contract or employment, regardless of when entered into, or under a substitute, directly or indirectly, for such contract or employment, including, without limiting the foregoing, a contract or employment with an employer or contracting party entered into within**

**ANALYSIS**

manager's commission may range from a low of 10% to a high of 25% or more depending on a number of factors which may include the manager's involvement in securing a record deal. The manager may, but is not obligated to, advance the artist funds for recording demonstration records. However, if a manager undertakes this responsibility (or what I consider to be a "monetary expression of faith" in the artist), he or she may rightfully request a higher commission of 20%. More established artists may be able to negotiate a lower commission in the 10%–15% range. In this contract the commission rate is applied against all gross income of the artist. Although for new artists, the commission is usually based on gross income, in some situations, certain items of gross income may be excluded before calculation of the commission. Usually this occurs in instances where the artist has more clout and in such a case, income that is used to offset definite expenses, such as recording costs, may be excluded before determining the commissionable income. Note that in this contract any shares of property or stock paid the artist as compensation is also deemed "income" and therefore subject to the manager's commission. An example of the importance of the inclusion of this sentence in the contract occurred recently when several artists including Alanis Morrisette and Master P agreed to endorse the company MP-3, which allows customers to download songs from the internet. Instead of receiv-

## CONTRACT

**six (6) months of the termination of a previous contract or employment if such previous contract or employment is commissionable hereunder, and any and all judgments, awards, settlements, payments, damages and proceeds (whenever received) relating to any suits, claims, actions, proceedings or arbitration proceedings arising out of any alleged breach of non-performance by others of any portion of any contracts, engagements, commitments or other agreements referred to in this Paragraph 6, all of which regardless of when entered into, when performed and when effective. Any Commissions or other sums due Manager resulting from any and all such judgments, awards, settlements, payments, damages and/or proceeds relating to any such suits, claims, actions, proceedings or arbitration proceedings shall be computed after first deducting counsel fees and disbursements, and any counsel fees and disbursements therefrom shall be paid by Artist. Notwithstanding anything to the contrary contained in this Agreement, as to any motion picture, phonograph record, film, tape, wire, transcription, recording or other reproduction of any of Artist's activities in the entertainment industries or resulting therefrom which is created in whole or in part during the Term hereof (or thereafter pursuant to an engagement, contract or agreement subject to Commission hereunder), Manager's Commission shall con-**

## ANALYSIS

ing a cash payment, MP-3 compensated these artists with shares of stock in their privately held company. Well, on the first day of trading on the stock market these shares more than quadrupled in value, and resulted in substantial earnings to the artists as they sold the shares at these high prices. Under the terms of this contract the manager would be entitled to his or her portion of shares as a commision. So, don't think this sentence has no value. Of course, the manager would like the definition of commissionable income to be as broad as possible, while the artist's representative should attempt to narrow its scope as much as possible.

| CONTRACT | ANALYSIS |
| --- | --- |
| tinue for so long as any of same are used, sold, leased, or otherwise exploited, whether during or after the Term hereof. Manager's Commissions shall, at Manager's option hereunder, apply to any monies paid to Artist by any employer of Artist as travel or living expenses in connection with any engagements, employment or agreement performed, secured or entered into by Artist.<br><br>(b) Expiration of the Term of this Agreement shall not affect Manager's right to receive Commissions for the full duration thereof with respect to agreements, engagements and commitments negotiated or entered into or renewed (in whole or in part) during the Term of this Agreement or any renewals or extensions thereof or substitutions therefor during or after the Term hereof. As used in this Agreement, "Artist" shall include any corporation, partnership, trust and/or other business entity of any kind or nature owned (partly or wholly) or controlled (directly or indirectly) by Artist or any members of Artist's family, and Artist agrees to cause any such corporation, partnership, trust and/or other business entity ("Firms") to enter into an agreement with Manager on the same terms as contained herein. Artist agrees that all gross monies or other considerations directly or indirectly earned or received by such Firms, in whole or in part, in con- | |

**CONTRACT**

nection with Artist's activities in the entertainment industry shall be subject to Commissions hereunder. Any agreement with each such Firm shall provide that such Firm has a right to furnish Artist's services on the terms and conditions set forth in this Agreement and the Firm shall become a signatory to this Agreement or one identical hereto. Artist shall (and hereby does) personally guarantee the obligations of any such Firm under this or any other agreement such Firm may have with Manager or any of Manager's affiliates. In the event Artist receives, as all or a part of Artist's compensation for activities hereunder, stock or rights to buy stock in any corporation or if Artist becomes the owner or packager of any entertainment property, regardless of the form of such ownership or packaging interest, the percentage compensation hereunder shall apply to such interest, and Manager shall be entitled to appropriate percentage of such interest. Notwithstanding the foregoing, Commissions hereunder shall not apply to union "scale" income received by Artist in connection with services as a non-featured side musician appearing on recordings or personal appearances of other (featured) artists unless Artist serves in royalty-earning and/or proprietary, controlling, ownership or partnership capacity in connection with such services, appearance or recording.

7. All expenses, other than normal

**ANALYSIS**

7. The manager shall be paid

**CONTRACT**

**minimum office overhead expenses, incurred by Manager on behalf of Artist (including, without limitation, long distance telephone calls, messenger fees, transportation and expenses while travelling, and promotion and publicity expenses) shall be promptly paid or reimbursed to Manager by Artist. Unless made reasonably necessary due to circumstances substantially outside of Manager's control, Manager shall not incur any single such expense in excess of Three Thousand Dollars ($3,000.00) without Artist's prior approval. Neither Manager nor any individual affiliated with Manager shall be required to travel to meet with Artist at any particular time or place, provided, however, that if Manager or any such individual employee of Manager does travel on behalf of Artist, then the cost of such travel and any and all expenses relating thereto shall be promptly paid or reimbursed by Artist. Notwithstanding anything to the contrary continued in this Paragraph 7, if the presence of Manager or any such individual is required outside the metropolitan area of [Artist's City] or City of New York, Artist agrees that Artist will pay for the expenses incurred, such expenses to consist of first class living accommodations and requirements (including any and all tips and incidentals) and travelling expenses. All such expenses incurred on Artist's behalf are to be paid in advance from Artist's accounts and**

**ANALYSIS**

promptly or reimbursed for all expenses, other than normal office overhead expenses incurred on behalf of the artist. However, the manager should have a certain dollar limit (in this contract, it's $3,000, which, in my opinion, is high for a new artist) above which he/she must obtain the approval of the artist before spending on the artist's behalf. Usually, all costs of the manager's travel (1st class or coach?) and incidental charges are to be reimbursed, as well as telephone charges, copying and other reasonable business expenses incurred on the artist's behalf. I strongly urge the artist to insist that the manager document these expenses and submit such charges to the artist on a regular basis.

**CONTRACT** | **ANALYSIS**

expense statements are to be turned in by Manager after each trip. Artist understands and agrees that Manager will not be able to turn in receipts for many of the expenses incurred by Manager in the course of doing Artist's business and therefor in such cases where Manager is unable to obtain receipts, Manager's statement to Artist in writing shall be deemed to be proof of such expense. In the event Manager has to entertain any individual or group of individuals anywhere in the world on Artist's behalf, Manager shall have the right to deduct such expenses as Manager incurs from Artist's accounts and in the event the accounts Manager holds for Artist are not sufficient to repay or advance the needed money to Manager, Artist shall promptly reimburse Manager or advance such money to Manager from the accounts of Artist that Artist holds upon Manager's request to Artist for such monies.

8. This Agreement shall not constitute a joint venture by or partnership between Manager and Artist, it being understood that Manager is acting hereunder as an independent contractor and that Manager may appoint or engage other persons or entities to perform any of the services required hereunder.

9. It is understood and agreed that Manager shall not be held in any way liable or responsible for any breach of contract or act or omis-

**CONTRACT**

**sion on the part of any person, firm or corporation with whom any engagement or contract of any kind is entered into by or for Artist for any reason.**

**10. Artist acknowledges that it is difficult to determine the amount and exact nature of services Manager must render hereunder at Artist's request. Accordingly, but without limitation of the foregoing, it is agreed that Manager shall not be deemed in breach of any Manager's obligations hereunder unless and until Artist shall give Manager written notice, by prepaid certified mail, return receipt requested, of the precise breach alleged and Manager fails, within thirty (30) days after receipt of such notice, to cure the breach specified by Artist, but only if cure thereof within such period is reasonable in view of the nature thereof and Manager's other responsibilities and obligations. In the event that the said cure cannot reasonably be completed within thirty (30) days, then in such event Manager shall not be deemed in breach if Manager shall have commenced such cure in good faith within said thirty (30) day period.**

**11. From time to time during the Term of this Agreement, Manager or other persons or entities owned and/or controlled directly or indirectly by Manager, or Manager's partners, shareholders, officers, directors and employees, whether**

**ANALYSIS**

11. This paragraph is a very important part of this contract, for the production company owner, who, as a result of the relationship being across the board is also the artist's co-publisher and manager. It says simply, if the manager owns a company which

## CONTRACT

**acting alone or in association with others, may package an entertainment program in which Artist is employed as an artist, or may act as the entrepreneur or promoter of an entertainment program in which Artist is employed as an artist, or may employ Artist in connection with the production of phonograph records, or as a songwriter, composer, arranger or otherwise in connection with the creation of literary or musical works. Such activity on Manager's or their part shall not be deemed to be a breach of this Agreement or of Manager's fiduciary obligations and duties to Artist, and such activity shall not in any way affect Manager's right to Commissions hereunder in all instances except as hereinafter specifically provided. Manager shall not be entitled to Commissions from Artist in connection with any gross monies or other considerations derived by Artist from (i) any employment or agreement hereunder where Artist is employed or engaged by Manager or by any person, firm or corporation owned or controlled by Manager, or by any of Manager's partners, shareholders, officers, directors or employees, in any capacity (including, without limitation, as the package agent for the entertainment program in which Artist is so employed or engaged, as Artist's music or literary publisher, or as Artist's record or promotion company); (ii) the sale, license or grant of any literary or musical rights to**

## ANALYSIS

also has a contract with the artist for, among other things, recording or publishing, any income earned by the artist from these other ventures shall not be subject to the manager's commission. This clause may allow the production company/publisher/manager's "Across The Board" interests to be validated. It acknowledges that the production company's interest in recording and publishing, in addition to managing the artist, is not considered a breach of the manager's fiduciary duty. Once a manager enters into a contract with an artist, he or she undertakes a fiduciary obligation to put the artist's interest above all else, even the manager's interest. This obligation is at the heart of the manager/artist relationship and a provision such as this is inserted to document the manager's agreement not to "double dip" or profit from being the owner of businesses involved in the artist's recording and publishing activities while also commissioning the earnings of the artist in these areas. If a manager attempts to "double dip," the manager clearly is protecting his or her interests first and not the artist's. If that's the case, an artist may ask a court to invalidate all agreements he or she has with the manager based on the theory of breach of the manager's fiduciary obligation to the artist. By inserting this provision in the management contract, the manager is agreeing not to commission the artist's income earned from companies in which the manager already has a financial stake. Therefore, the manager, who signs an artist "Across The Board," cannot

**CONTRACT**

**Manager or any person, firm or corporation owned or controlled by Manager.**

**12. This Agreement shall be deemed to have been made in the State of New York and its validity, construction, performance and breach shall be governed by the laws of the State of New York applicable to agreements made and to be wholly performed therein. Artist agrees to submit to the jurisdiction of the Federal or State courts located in New York City in any action which may arise out of this Agreement and said courts shall have exclusive jurisdiction over all disputes between Manager and Artist pertaining to this Agreement and all matters related thereto. Nothing contained herein shall constitute a waiver of any other remedies available to Manager. Nothing contained in this Paragraph 12 shall preclude Manager from joining Artist in an action brought by a third party against Manager in any jurisdiction, although Manager's failure to join Artist in any such action in one instance shall not constitute a waiver of any of Manager's rights with respect thereto, or with respect to any subsequent action brought by a third party against Manager.**

**13. Artist hereby represents and**

**ANALYSIS**

commission recording, publishing or songwriter's advances or royalties and usually ends up being able to commission only the income generated by activities such as the artist's personal performances, endorsements and other non-record or publishing activities.

12. The parties have the right to have the agreement construed under the laws of a particular state. In most entertainment contracts, the parties agree to be bound under the laws of a state where a great deal of entertainment law court decisions or state regulations exist. New York or California are two of the most popular states in this regard. This agreement stipulates that the courts of the state of New York shall have jurisdiction of and be the proper venue for any disputes.

| CONTRACT | ANALYSIS |
|---|---|
| warrants that Artist has not entered into any agreements or contracts which shall or do in any way interfere or conflict with Artist's obligations, promises and/or warranties hereunder and that Artist is free to enter into this Agreement, and Artist agrees to indemnify and hold Manager harmless from any loss, cost or liability (including reasonable attorneys' fees) as a result of any breach by Artist of any of Artist's representations, warranties or covenants contained herein, including, without limitation, the provisions of Paragraph 9 hereof.<br><br>14. The services rendered by Artist are special, unique and irreplaceable, and any breach or threatened breach by Artist of any of Artist's obligations hereunder may be enjoined temporarily or permanently without regard to and without limiting any other remedy that may be available to Manager.<br><br>15. In the event Manager (or Manager's successors and/or assigns, if any) shall assign or otherwise transfer this Agreement or any of Manager's (or their) rights hereunder to any corporation, entity or partnership (which Manager shall only have the right to do provided that [Name of Key Person in Production/Management Company] is a shareholder, partner, or employee thereof) or in the event Manager shall delegate any of Manager's (or their) obligations hereunder, in whole or in part, to any party(ies) at | |

**CONTRACT** | **ANALYSIS**

any time comprising Manager or any corporation owned by Manager (or them) or any of such parties in whole or in part, such assignment shall be (and hereby is) approved and accepted and deemed to be a novation of this Agreement. Artist shall not have the right to assign any of Artist's rights or delegate any of Artist's obligations hereunder. Without in any way derogating from the preceding sentence, this Agreement shall inure to the benefit of and be binding upon each of the parties hereto and their respective successors, assigns, heirs, executors, administrators and legal and personal representatives.

16. Any notice given hereunder shall be sufficient only if mailed via certified mail, return receipt requested, postage prepaid, and if to Manager, addressed to Manager at the address hereinabove specified, with a copy to [Production/Management Company Attorney's Name and Address], and any other address(es) of which Artist has been given notice as provided herein, and if to Artist, at Artist's last known address(es) or the following address or any other address(es) of which Manager has been given notice as provided herein: [Artist's Attorney's Name and Address]. Any notice shall be effective as of the date three (3) days after mailing as aforesaid in the continental United States except for notices of change in ad-

**CONTRACT** | **ANALYSIS**

dress (which shall only be effective on receipt).

17. Nothing in this Agreement shall be construed so as to require the commission of any act contrary to law. Wherever there is any conflict between the provisions of this Agreement and any present or future statute, law, ordinance or regulation the latter shall prevail, but in such event the provision(s) of this Agreement affected shall be curtailed or limited only to the minimum extent necessary to bring it within the requirements of the latter. (The parties hereto do not intend by the foregoing sentence to imply the illegality, voidness or unenforceability of any term, provision or paragraph of this Agreement).

18. This Agreement sets forth the entire agreement between the parties hereto, and replaces and supersedes all other agreements relating to the subject matter hereof. This Agreement cannot be modified, altered, terminated or otherwise changed except by an agreement in writing signed by the parties hereto. In the event that any party hereto initiates litigation to enforce this Agreement, the party prevailing to the greater extent shall be entitled to recover reasonable attorneys' fees and costs reasonably incurred in connection with such litigation. No waiver of any provision of this contract or of any default hereunder shall affect Man-

| CONTRACT | ANALYSIS |
| --- | --- |
| ager's rights thereafter to enforce such provision or to exercise any right or remedy in the event of any other default, whether or not similar. | |
| 19. If necessary in Manager's good faith opinion to ensure Manager of payments for Manager's services as provided herein, Artist agrees to deliver to Manager a written assignment of so much of Artist's compensation from any source as hereinabove agreed upon to be Manager's compensation, and if not so delivered to Manager, Manager is authorized to draw an assignment to Manager for such salary, execute the same in the name of Artist and collect therefrom with the same force and effect as though signed by Artist in person, or to require any party paying such compensation directly or indirectly to Artist to pay the same over to Manager, in which event this instrument or a copy thereof shall be authority for such employer to make such deductions and payment. All the terms and conditions of this Agreement shall be irrevocable, this Agreement constituting a contract and a power of attorney and creating an agency coupled with an interest. | 19. In this paragraph the manager is allowed, in his or her "good faith opinion" to request the artist to assign the right to compensation to the manager. It further states if the artist fails to so assign this right, the manager is empowered to effect such an assignment on their own. What it means, of course, is that the manager may request to be the first point of receipt of funds paid for the artist's services, which enables the manager to protect his or her right to receive commissions. |
| 20. Artist hereby expressly agrees that Artist will not at any time, without Manager's express written consent, exert or permit any third party to exert any of the powers herein granted to Manager so as to | |

**CONTRACT**

**ANALYSIS**

create any confusion or conflict of authority in the mind of any third person. Artist understands and agrees that Manager's interest and compensation under this Agreement shall be a continuing interest and shall not be revocable in any event or for any reason whatsoever for the term of this Agreement and any extension(s), renewal(s), replacement(s) or substitution(s) thereof, except only as specified in this Agreement.

21. Manager shall have the right to advertise and publicize Manager as Artist's exclusive personal manager and representative and Artist shall cooperate and assist Manager in securing written (and, if applicable, logo) credit as such wherever reasonably possible.

22. Artist acknowledges that no promises, representations or inducements have been made by Manager or on Manager's behalf, except as specifically set forth herein, and Artist further acknowledges that Manager's acceptance and execution hereof is in reliance on this fact.

23. Artist hereby represents, warrants and agrees that Artist shall cooperate fully with Manager in any and all of Manager's efforts to comply with any laws as same may apply to the manner in which Manager conducts Manager's management business generally and/or as it specifically pertains to Artist and/or

**CONTRACT**

**the rendition of Manager's services hereunder. Artist hereby further agrees to negotiate with Manager in good faith regarding any and all amendments which may be required to be made to this Agreement in order to conform to the requirements of any laws and/or in order to continue the personal manager relationship created hereby. Artist hereby acknowledges that Manager has advised Artist that Manager shares common ownership with [Production Company's Name], the record company with whom Artist is simultaneously entering into a recording agreement. Manager has advised Artist and Artist hereby agrees to obtain independent legal counsel to negotiate with [Production Company's Name] and to represent Artist regarding Artist's activities with [Production Company's Name].**

**24. Manager shall be entitled (but in no event shall be obligated) to secure, in Manager's own name or otherwise and at Manager's expense, life, accident, health and/or other insurance covering Artist, either independently or together with Manager or any party Manager designates being the sole beneficiary thereof and neither Artist nor Artist's estate shall have any right, title or interest in and to such insurance or any proceeds therefrom. Artist shall cooperate fully with Manager in connection with the obtaining of such insurance, if**

**ANALYSIS**

24. Most managers' contracts also contain a provision which allows the manager to obtain a life insurance policy on the artist and be named the payee should the artist meet an untimely death. I generally resent these provisions because they give me cause to believe that an unscrupulous manager, at some point, may find it more beneficial to have the artist dead than alive. However, it is reasonable to believe that a reputable manager has a vested financial interest in the artist's continued ability to perform. It's been reported that Tony Bennett, the legendary performer who's in his seven-

**CONTRACT**

**any, including, without limitation, by timely submitting to medical examinations and by completing any and all documents necessary or desirable in respect thereof.**

**25. (a) This Agreement shall apply to each member of Artist jointly and individually. Accordingly, whenever the word "Artist" is used in this Agreement, it shall mean, except as otherwise expressly provided, each member of Artist jointly and severally. In the event that any member of Artist engages in any activities in the entertainment or publishing industries separate and apart from Artist as a group, this Agreement shall nonetheless apply and all the terms and conditions of this Agreement shall be applicable to such activities.**

**(b) Artist represents and warrants that following the date hereof, no individual shall become a member of Artist or otherwise ("New Member") until Artist has obtained Manager's prior consent. In this connection (A) any such New Member shall be automatically bound by all of the terms and conditions of this Agreement as if such New Member had executed this Agreement on the date hereof, and (B) Artist shall cause each such New Member to execute and deliver to Manager any and all documents which Manager deems necessary or expedient to evidence the foregoing, including without limi-**

**ANALYSIS**

ties, is booked solid for performances two or three years in advance. Should he pass prior to fulfilling the engagements, his manager, who is also his son, would take a severe financial loss and therefore should be allowed to protect his interests with a life insurance policy on this important client.

25. If the artist is a group, the manager may also have legitimate concerns about who comprises the group. Therefore, a provision binding members of the group, whether the group stays intact or disbands, is reasonable. If a member is replaced, a manager may also want the right to approve the replacement, who shall also be required to execute a similar management contract with the manager.

**CONTRACT** | **ANALYSIS**

tation, any agreement with Manager containing the same terms and conditions set forth herein, but Manager's rights hereunder shall not be diminished by any such approved New Member's failure or refusal to execute such agreement.

(c) Each person leaving, or ceasing to perform with the group, for any reason whatsoever (i) shall be bound by all the terms and conditions of this Agreement as though said leaving member(s) individually executed this Agreement and (ii) shall relinquish all of his or her rights, of any nature whatsoever (including but not limited to trademark, servicemark, etc.) in the group name to the remaining persons comprising Artist. In the event this Agreement is terminated prior to the expiration date hereof, including any renewal or extension period for any reason whatsoever, as to any person designated herein as "Artist", such termination shall not affect the continuing force and validity of each and all other persons designated as "Artist" herein.

(d) In the event that any individual(s) at any time comprising Artist do not execute this Agreement, it shall nonetheless be binding upon the individual(s) who have at any time signed it (in counterparts or all on one copy) as if only such individual(s) were listed on the first and last pages hereof.

26. If and to the extent that "Artist"

CONTRACT | ANALYSIS

at any time refers in whole or in part to a female artist, the words used herein to designate such artist that have been used in the masculine gender shall be deemed to have been used in the feminine gender.

27. Artist specifically acknowledges that this Agreement is executed as an arm's length transaction, separate and apart from any fiduciary or other duty or obligation of any kind or nature which may be owed by Manager or any affiliate of Manager to Artist, and that Manager is under not such duty or obligation to Artist in connection with this Agreement, whether or not Manager or any affiliate or Manager now has or at any time had had any fiduciary or other relationship of any kind or nature with Artist. It is specifically understood and agreed that Artist is free to utilize separate, independent legal counsel to advise Artist with respect to the respective rights and obligations of each party under this Agreement, any failure by Artist to seek or obtain such legal counsel to be Artist's sole choice (and contrary to Manager's wishes).

IN WITNESS WHEREOF, the parties hereunder set their hands and seals on the day and year first above written.

[Name of Management Company]

______________________________

**CONTRACT**

An Authorized Signer

---

Artist

**IMPORTANT LEGAL DOCUMENT—CONSULT YOUR OWN ATTORNEY BEFORE SIGNING**

**ANALYSIS**

13

# Statement and Analysis of Management Earnings

## *Maximizing the Earnings of the Artist*

In order to provide an effective analysis of management earnings, it is necessary to base the analysis on the activities of a fictitious artist. Let's suppose the artist is multitalented. He or she has a unique look or style which is attractive to certain product endorser's ("endorsements"), produces music for other artists as well as themselves ("third-party producer activities"), and is in demand for live performances ("live performances") and appearances in movies ("movie roles"). As a result, the artist is capable of generating income from at least four different sources in addition to his or her recording and songwriting activities.

Once the performer is signed with the production company, who also acts as the performer's manager in an across the deal arrangement, the management division of the production company cannot commission the artist's earnings from recording, songwriting, or publishing activities. However, if the artist is contracted for lucrative endorsements, third party producer activities, live performances, and movie roles, the earnings generated by these activities may be subject to commission by the manager.

In our model, we will deal with four types of artist activities where the earnings of the artist could be commissioned.

## LIVE PERFORMANCES

First, if the artist has a successful record, it is likely she or he will obtain live performance engagements. If the artist performs 50 engagements at a fee of $5,000 per date, the manager will be entitled to $50,000 in commissions.

| *Artist's Gross Earnings* | *Management Commission (20% of Gross)* |
| --- | --- |
| Artist performs fifty (50) dates at $5,000 per date<br>50 x $5,000 = $250,000 gross | $50,000 |

## THIRD-PARTY PRODUCER ACTIVITIES

Second, if the artist produces five master recordings for $15,000 per recording for other acts not signed to the production company, the manager's commission on the $75,000 of income will be $15,000.

| *Artist's Gross Earnings* | *Management Commission (20% of Gross)* |
| --- | --- |
| Artist/producer produces five (5) master recordings (sides) for parties other than the production company at $15,000 per side<br>5 x $15,000 = $75,000 gross | $15,000 |

## ENDORSEMENTS

As a result of the artist's unique look and popularity, the manager is able to arrange an agreement with a toothpaste company, who wants to use the artist in national radio or TV commercials promoting their product. The deal calls for the payment of a fee of $100,000 to the artist. Of course, the manager's 20% commission amounts to $20,000.

| *Commissioned Activity* | *Management Commission* |
|---|---|
| Artist endorses product (toothpaste commercial) One-time payment of $100,000 | $20,000 |

## MOVIE ROLES

If the artist has some acting talents, it is possible for the manager to arrange for his or her appearance in a motion picture. This medium is becoming increasingly popular for rap artists. While the fee for a cameo appearance or a featured role can range from $75,000 to $1 million, depending on the leverage of the artist, the time it takes to perform in a movie may be able to be scheduled so it does not interfere with the artist's recording or live performance schedule. In our case, let's suppose the artist makes a featured performance in a movie for a flat fee of $100,000. In addition to providing both the artist and the manager with important earnings beyond recording and publishing, the exposure of the artist can greatly enhance his or her image as well as promote the artist's musical career.

| *Artist's Gross Earnings* | *Management Commission (20% of Gross)* |
|---|---|
| Artist performs featured role in a motion picture One-time flat fee of $100,000 | $20,000 |

While I vehemently decry and protest the recent changes in recording agreements as I alluded to earlier, which make it almost impossible for the artist to earn anything other than advances for recording services, the potential for earnings from the exploitation of the artist's other talents is enhanced by the success of record sales and should not be overlooked.

In today's popular culture, where any publicity is considered good publicity, artists who achieve success in music will find themselves in a great position to generate additional earnings from other sources such as advertisers, movie companies, clothing manufacturers, and so on.

You see from the example that a successful artist should generate income from as many sources as benefit the development of his or her career. One exceptionally talented artist can become a self-sustaining business entity of its own, generating substantial income for the manager who fully exploits all of the artist's opportunities and the manager may generate substantial income as a result of representing an exceptionally talented artist.

14

# Incorporating the Information

Some might consider the first part of this book the easy material. You've gone through the contracts and reviewed the analysis. Hopefully, you've gotten an answer to a question that's puzzled you for a while and maybe even caused procrastination or problems. You've read and reread about the importance of applying keys for success, the Three Big P's, structuring the relationship of the players involved, and details about people in the business. Now it's time to take what you've read and begin to incorporate the information into your business frame and frame of mind.

Whether you're about to begin your business or are in the process of reorganizing, now is the time to apply the information and make it work for you. Reread the section on choosing the proper business structure. If you have questions, write them down and meet with a professional who is qualified to give you answers. Yes, it will cost you. But the cost of charges for a professional (an attorney or accountant) in the early stages of your career to get advice is miniscule when compared with the amount of time and earnings that can be lost (or not flowing to your account!) if your contracts are not designed to work in your best interest. Having the right foundation can make the difference in both the short and long run. Make certain you have your business plan written down so that your focus is clear to you and anyone you intend to do business with. The contracts are there for you to review at any time—that's why you bought the book. Take the time to do a mental review and think about how to adapt the basic structures to your situation. Again, if you have questions, seek advice. Remember, the contracts are samples and should be used only as guidelines to what is going on in the legal end of the music business. Don't do yourself a disservice by trying to evaluate and make actual changes or assume that you will be able to apply them to your particular situation. It may appear simple, but as I've pointed out earlier, the fine print is not to be taken lightly—remember, your business is at stake and the stakes in this business are high.

When you meet with your professional advisers or your partners or if you choose to work independently while you are structuring your business, keep in mind the importance of diversifying your income. Take advantage of the available markets (mutual funds, stocks, IRAs, etc.). Find out what's available and get your money involved to work for your future while your music is working for you now and in the future.

I have to reiterate the importance of education. Read, read, read. Know what's going on in the entertainment business and in the world. You'll be surprised to find out how closely related all movements in business in general impact the music business.

As you read the last section of this book, keep in mind that it encapsulates situations and ideas. Read through these last pages and be ready to move your business forward and create the best of times in the music industry.

## SUMMARY

# Moving You and Your Business into the Future

We've finished the review of the contracts and the general concept of how to take care of your business. Now it's time to understand how to move forward with strategies for success for your future in the music business.

The truly talented can make a living in the music industry if they have perseverance and determination. Take, for example, the major talents I've associated with over the years; two I represent and one I've performed with. Each one has been a true testament to my belief. In the late 1960s, the O'Jays lived around the corner from my childhood home in Cleveland, Ohio, with one of their relatives. The neighborhood was great, but it wasn't the music capitol of the world. Times were hard in the record business and I'm sure The O'Jays—like the rest of us—were having a difficult time making ends meet. But they persevered and captivated audiences at the legendary Leo's Casino in Cleveland, the Uptown in Philly, and the Regal in Chicago. Wherever they performed they made their smooth love song, "Look Over Your Shoulder," and the dance hit, "One Night Affair," come alive in the hearts and minds of the audience. In 1972,

Gamble & Huff signed The O'Jays to their Philadelphia International Records label (which was distributed by Columbia Records and run, at that time, by Clive Davis). They saw to it The O'Jays got their just due and the hit records started with "Backstabbers" and "Love Train" and continued with "Used to Be My Girl" and "For the Love of Money."

Then there was Larry Blackmon. Years before there was Cameo, Larry had a group called The New York City Players. They played on what was commonly referred to in the business as the "chitlin' circuit," which was a small network of clubs in the United States and Canada that featured, on a weekly basis, predominantly black performing acts. The "circuit" was a grind but it kept the groups busy and on bus tours in order to make dates. My group, The New Decade, made the tour as well until I joined Cameo shortly after it was formed in 1976. It was during my brief work with Larry's group that I made the decision to get a law degree in order to best protect and advance my musical career. The demands of law school kept me from being a part of the eventual musical success I knew had to and would happen for Cameo (because Larry had overdrive!) but I moved forward with no regrets. With hard work and determination, success occurred for them in a huge way in 1987 with their international hit, "Word Up."

Lastly, I have to mention Gerald Levert. Many people probably think he had it made because of his father, Eddie Levert, lead singer of The O'Jays. What people don't know is that it took two years of performing in small clubs, writing songs, and perfecting his skills while he was still in high school. During that time, his group, Levert, released an album on Network Records, an independent record label owned by Harry Coombs, former VP of Marketing for Philadelphia International Records. They were soon signed by Hank Caldwell, VP of Black Music at Atlantic Records and had their first hit, "Pop Pop Pop Goes My Mind."

We know each of these people all had (and still have!) talent. And I know they wouldn't have survived without powerful product, proper perspective, and professional attitude (Determination helped quite a bit, too!)—all factors necessary for achieving complete success in today's music industry.

Having grown up during the era of "soul music" and "funk" bands, I was influenced and inspired by tremendous songwriters and performers such as Curtis Mayfield, Marvin Gaye, and Stevie Wonder, and I can personally affirm the inspirational qualities of music. I contend, at least from my experience, that "people gotta have it"—"it" being music that moves the body and the soul, confirming my belief that music has been and will always be a primary source of spiritual uplift and social entertainment for the masses.

**In the new millennium, the scope and breadth of the entire entertainment business will increase exponentially.**

In the new millennium, the scope and breadth of the entire entertainment business will increase exponentially. Commentators have already noted the effect entertainment is having on all businesses in general. In these times when the economy is at an all-time high and unemployment is at its lowest point in a generation, everyone wants to be entertained, in some form or fashion, during their every waking hour. I've seen music become totally pervasive: there's mood music in stores to encourage sales from the hip-hop beats on high volume in the sneaker section, to the sensuous love melodies for choosing lingerie. Even the most staid banking and financial institutions are attempting to "lighten up" by incorporating certain aspects of entertainment into their marketing schemes. Have you noticed the new cartoon graphics on many of the ATM machines you use? You can bet you'll soon be hearing a hip-hop audiotrack to accompany these exciting visuals. It makes taking money out (and depleting your balance) an experience you're more apt to enjoy with the excitement of music. So what does this say to the individual with creative musical or other talents? It says—loud and clear, confirming what I know to be true—these are great times to be in this business.

For the creative person the future holds the potential to provide unlimited wealth and success. However, just as in the past, having knowledge of how the business works is essential, but it is not always enough. You not only have to know how to TCB (Take Care of Business), you also have to be dedicated to knowing how to SIB (Stay in Business). As the business world changes be confident that you can change with it. Everyone should learn and apply new skills and be able to step in at a moment's notice to do a job no one thought could be done. The ability to TCB and SIB will be even more promising if you understand and apply the Three Big P's and recognize their importance in the future of the ever-growing and ever-changing entertainment business.

## POWERFUL PRODUCT AND THE FUTURE

Powerful product will be just as important in the future as it is now, not only as background music for ATM graphics or selling merchandise in department stores, but also as a tool to generate sales for the artist's share of the millions of dollars that can be gained from worldwide record sales. Business will be changing hands in a New York second with people in all realms of business creating powerful products and knowing how to move them. Each change will come at the speed of the fastest computers and their downloading capabilities. We'll find more often that artists will be reaching (and selling product in) China, Paris, and Mexico with their buyers hitting "Enter" on the keyboard.

For those in the music industry, the focus in the future will not only be on the powerful products created but also the effect of new inventions, which will help sell products. This means you have to be able to cross-promote. In order to do this, creative talent must develop a synergistic approach to the exploitation of talent through various media outlets; a recording artist, for example, could consider creating another powerful product by honing acting skills, a lyricist might want to investigate writing screen plays, and record producers could try their hand at producing and directing television shows. A number of recording stars, such as Brandy, Ice Cube, Usher, and Master P are already continuing the pattern set by earlier recording stars like Diana

Ross, Meatloaf, and Willie Nelson, each of whom knew the importance of SIB. Those artists mastered their "acting chops" for important cross-promotional activities in motion pictures and TV.

It's also important for recording stars to note the success of artists like rap star, Queen Latifah and singer Jewel, who not only perform on records, but also, star in movies, write books, and, in the case of Queen Latifah, develop and star in a talk show. For Latifah, all this is in addition to running a successful record production company. She is definitely focused on creating a totally synergistic plan to TCB and SIB! Another paradigm is the broadway star and tap dance genius, Savion Glover, an entertainer who has taken his powerful stage performing product to another studio by recording a tap dance solo on a CD by Prince. He's done what I call "morphing," being able to move from one career to another, which is in my opinion, the key to SIB. Is the opportunity there? You bet. What you have to do in order to succeed is think of your business (yourself) as a product that can transform and restyle with time, while creating current and future earnings.

There is no doubt that changes will inadvertently make taking care of your music business easier because of the introduction of new and effective technological products that have been developed in recent years. Each of these advances will greatly enhance an artist's ability to create and exploit her or his powerful product. One major change has already occurred with reduction in the price of (and the increase in the widespread use of) digital recorders and samplers. This alone has drastically cut the costs of recording and has enhanced the recording capability for many artists who were not able to afford expensive studio rates and the cost of hiring live musicians. While there currently seems to be a backlash against artists whose recordings are composed solely of synthesized sound, the use of live musicians (other than rhythm sections) is more likely a thing of the past. When you consider the high quality of synthesizer sounds, which provide horn and string accompaniment, rivaling those created by real musicians, it's easy to understand it's a product whose time has come.

The methods in which music will be exploited and delivered to consumers will also have a profound effect on your powerful product. Advanced computer technology combined with the scope of the Internet is creating new and exciting means of marketing and delivering powerful product to the marketplace. One of the most promising technological advances in the music industry recently involves a creation called MP-3. MP-3 is a system that can be purchased online and allows music to be downloaded from the Internet to an individual computer, which can then be transferred to portable MP-3 players for personal use. This computer software program transforms a normal digitized song into a highly compressed format, allowing near CD-quality music which can be stored on the hard drive. Of course, like most new technological advances of the past that were introduced to conventional markets, it's causing quite an uproar from various factions of the music industry. On the one hand, artists are heralding this technology as the key to allowing them to market their music from their studios, directly to consumers, via the Internet. On the other side there are the major labels who are concerned, and rightfully so, that they will surely lose significant dollars if they don't have a way to protect their copyrights from the vast exploitation of music creation and sales over which they have no control. To make this technological advance equitable to both sides, various parties in the music industry are currently trying to develop systems to mark and thereby control or monitor the dissemination of product so there is benefit for the interests of everyone involved.

Enhanced CDs are another promising direct marketing approach to buyers. Not only do they contain audio tracks, but there are also visual programs which can be displayed on the computer monitor. These visual programs are much like recorded web sites that may include many pages of promotion, audio and video presentations of an artist, and any other products from the company's label which can be purchased by direct mail or from their Internet site. By buying one artist's CD, you have the opportunity to preview and order other artists' CDs with the single click of a mouse. Don't let the changes that are occurring in the industry or the new technology intimidate you. Move with it to move your business.

## KEEP YOUR PROPER PERSPECTIVE FOR THE FUTURE

As previously mentioned, consolidation is another phenomenon occurring in the entertainment industry. Not only is it having a major effect on the music industry as it relates to record companies, it is also affecting the live performance market. SFX Entertainment is one company that has recently emerged as a major "consolidator" in the area of concert promotion and venues. At the time of this writing, SFX owns, or operates under lease, seventy-three venues, including a number of amphitheaters in the top ten U.S. live performance markets. As indicated in a recent article from *Newsweek* magazine, "No single company has ever controlled so much of the live entertainment business." SFX has purchased most of the large concert promoters in the United States. The venture has caused many smaller promoters and booking agencies to express concern about the future of the live performance business. These promoters contend that the control exerted by SFX leases on venues throughout the country will lessen their ability to present shows in the most desirable concert halls and auditoriums. There are also the surviving independent booking agents who fear that SFX will (because of its power to approach live performers directly with the promise of a nationwide prepackaged tour in its venues) undercut and eliminate the need for booking agents.

Artists have valid concerns that a company with the control of SFX may eventually be able to dictate the price they receive from large tours by arguing "either you tour with us at X [their dollar] amount or you can't perform in our venues." This is a real problem for many artists because they know live performance may be as important to their success as recorded music. This is similar to what has occurred for certain national tours for R&B and jazz groups in recent years. The scenario is that a national promoter will pay (over the course of a multiweek tour) several big-name artists a weekly paycheck to perform together. Instead of receiving a date-by-date negotiated gross fee, out of which artists usually determine and control the band's salary and other travel costs, artists give up their control to a national promoter who bears the cost of all the expenses. If an artist balks at the proposed weekly fee, another artist is slotted to take her or his place. The artist with the complaint loses the opportunity to participate in the tour and promote product by performing live for fans. While the artist may be forced to work for less pay and with less control the need to promote their product and career may outweigh the potential drawbacks of this type of prepackaged tour. It is an option but not the only one available for entertainers. The definite upside to this new approach to touring is that it may create a more positive environment for the lesser known niche market acts smaller promoters and venues will undoubtedly be craving for in order to satisfy their live performance business. Artists with the foresight and determination to deliver good, solid, live performances on their own can and will be appreciated by the national audiences they'll build from touring small clubs through local promoters. As always, he or she who controls the powerful product will control his or her destiny. The popular musician and vocalist, Ani DiFranco, for example, built her independent record label from a mailing list of over fifty thousand names that were compiled while she toured small clubs over the years. Her label, Righteous Babe Records, is now a major player. In the future the controllers of their own powerful product will have to be aware of (and knowledgeable about) the new merchandise and technological advances available to market, sell, and otherwise exploit their music.

You must also recognize that the available avenues which were once standard in doing business are not being eliminated but are merely changing to meet the challenges of a new era. Consolidation and the resulting downsizing of major record labels will have a profound effect on the music business and will force everyone involved to develop (if they haven't by now) the "proper perspective." These two factors alone (consolidation and downsizing) will result in the narrowing of opportunities to affiliate with major record labels not only for the artists, but also for record company executives. Many will be forced to outline survival tactics to get them through. The change is in full swing, with the foundations of the recording industry giving way to new structures.

In 1998, the "Big Six" was reduced to the "Big Five," as Seagram, Inc., owner of the Universal Record Group (formerly MCA Music Entertainment Group) purchased Polygram Records for $10.6 billion. This created the largest record company in the world, with a worldwide market share of 23% and revenues of $6.1 billion annually! It has been reported that these companies, Polygram and Universal, will consolidate operations which could lead to $275 million to $300 million in cost savings. This brilliant business move will result in a leaner and meaner company, with fewer acts and a diminished executive roster (*read:* fewer opportunities for new developing acts). While it's no secret that up to 200 employees of the amalgamated Universal/Polygram conglomerate have been terminated and several acts will be dropped, you may be surprised to learn it's been rumored that the requisite for remaining acts to stay on board is that they must have had at least one certified gold LP out of the last two records they released. This seems to be based on an unwritten formula which states that major record labels must commit at least $1 million for each new act's CD release. This cost includes recording, manufacturing, distribution, and promotion. If the act doesn't sell at least 250,000 units, it may not be profitable for the major label to commit to recording another of the act's CDs.

The culprit driving the major labels' desire and need to sell a million in order to make millions is high overhead. While the double-edge sword of digital recording technology drastically reduces the actual costs of recording, it also allows the major labels to use this argument to justify lower advances to artists to record their products—a trend that will be accelerated upon completion of the consolidation process of the major labels, as the opportunities for new artist contracts will be few and far between. Needless to say, the record companies are preparing for the future of their business. In early 2000 Time Warner, Inc. (owner of WEA) and EMI proposed merging their respective music operations, creating what will (if approved) catapult the combined company's market share to second behind Universal Music Group and reducing the "Big Five" to the "Big Four." This announcement came on the heels of Time Warner, Inc. announcing a merger with America On Line (AOL), giving the combined firms significant strength in internet delivery capability.

With the upheaval of the well-established recording giants, some in the industry are in a panic. Then there are those of us who know there will always be a target market for various genres of music and money to be made for now and the future.

## DON'T MISS YOUR TARGET MARKET

You have to keep the proper perspective by continuously reevaluating the future of the record industry and knowing how to succeed in spite of the changes. Being mindful of the changing demographics and the aging population of the entire world (an entire world where people still "got to have it!") has to be a part of that perspective when planning your future business strategy and moving forward. Record companies have aimed their marketing efforts primarily at the 13- to 24-year-old market, ignoring the older 25- to 55-year-old market, which grew up on and made the current album/CD market flourish. As major label opportunities for new artists are reduced, A&R executives, many of whom are producers themselves, attempt to mold most of their artists into the same style, or adopt the sound of current air play hits. This drastically reduces the variety of new sounds and styles of music we, the buying public, hear on the radio and are able to buy in record stores.

We've noticed on country radio that older hit artists like Waylon Jennings and Johnny Cash receive no air play, and are replaced on the charts by younger artists such as Garth Brooks and Faith Hill. This trend seems to be spreading to urban stations as well, where hit acts like Luther Vandross, The O'Jays, and Patti Labelle have a hard time garnering spins on mainstream urban stations. As a result, a valuable, totally undeserved market of older radio listeners and CD buyers exist who are clamoring for new products from their old favorites and new artists who specialize in recording music that satisfies this market. The success of Santana's multiplatinum and Grammy winning album "Supernatural" is evidence of the demand for this type of product. As new solid gold and soul oldies radio formats are and will continue to flourish, the recording and programming of new material by these vintage artists is still lacking. Producers and writers have a wealth of talent available for them if they understand that they can sell product from exceptional talent—even if record companies aren't signing older artists—and make a profit. Artists and producers with the proper perspective will make use of any and all available talent to garner their market share.

Prince has led the way in resuscitating the recording career of greats like Chaka Khan and Larry Graham by allowing them to record in his studio and utilize a new distribution network he has helped to establish. Remember my earlier reference to the artist Ani DiFranco? Righteous Babe Records grew via her direct mail and independent sales, not a major record label. Instead of receiving the $1.00 to $1.25 artist royalty she would have been entitled to had she been signed with a major label, she made $5 to $6 after deducting costs by selling her music through her own company. Her story came to the attention of Prince, who after severing his long-standing contract with Warner Brothers Records, decided to sell his music directly to the public via the Internet and later through independent distributors. After selling over 250,000 units of his CD *Crystal Ball* via Internet marketing, he had to admit that he had never made so much money from the sale of any of his earlier CDs, which sold millions under his Warner Brothers deal.

On a recent talk show on Black Entertainment Television (BET), Larry Graham stated that he expected to earn $7 per unit from the sale of his new CD. At that rate, he would earn $1 million by selling just 150,000 units. Now that's not to say that the entire million dollars is profit. But, because he doesn't have a large staff or a number of other acts to invest in, he can retain a large percentage of the earnings. It is likely that other classic acts will follow suit once more artists understand what I've known for quite some time: that "you don't have to sell a million to make a million."

Record labels have experienced tremendous growth in the profit margins on CDs, which is now the predominant configuration for the sale of a recorded product. The growth is due, in part, to contractual provisions that clearly favor the record companies. These provisions allow the label's payout to artists and producers for the sale of CDs to be equal to, or, in certain circumstances, lower than that for cassettes. This is the practice even though the CDs wholesale and retail list prices are markedly higher than cassettes' and the manufacturing costs for CDs are lower than ever before. Record labels are also experiencing an all-time high in the amount of money generated from music sales (while units sales growth is flattening) and foreign sales of music products. While the domestic sale of music may not be growing by leaps and bounds, the sale of music by U.S. artists overseas is greater than ever. What does this spell? P-R-O-F-I-T for the record company. This is only bad news for artists looking for that major record label deal to get their career going. The reality is that the deal is more likely not going to be there. Why? Because if you aren't that one in a million act that can sell a million so the corporation can make millions, "foggedabodit." So, what's the alternative? Are you out of the business before you even get started because you may not fit the profile or sound of that "one in a million act"? Not if you have and keep the proper perspective, which is "You don't have to sell a million to make millions." I feel it will have to be adopted by all artists, entrepreneurs, and record company executives, who are interested in being a lucrative part of the music business in the new millennium.

## THE IMPORTANCE OF PROFESSIONAL ATTITUDE IN THE FUTURE

In the past, recording artists and other creative talents were not expected to display or possess the attributes of a professional beyond their performance in the studio or on a stage. However, many current performers not only possess the qualities of successful businesspersons, often bolstered by college degrees, but publicly espouse the benefits to be attained by projecting a positive, professional attitude (Motown trained their artists to project such an attitude.) Their recognition of the potential for success from cross-media exploitation of their talents encourages them to approach each new opportunity as a step toward achieving goals their predecessors only dreamed of. Sean "Puffy" Combs (who, by the way, attended Howard University) has used his fame and recognition to launch the franchising of his image in restaurants, clothing, a sports management agency, and several other ventures. Similarly, Percy Miller ("Master P") has used his basketball playing stint in the CBA (and trying out for the NBA's Charlotte Hornets) as a way to build his credibility with professional athletes. As a result, his No Limit Sports Agency has landed contracts to represent such stellar athletes as Heisman Trophy winner Ricky Williams. In addition to his No Limits record label and his Sports Agency, Master P has also made the foray into toy sales, with the licensing for the sale of the 16½" Master P dolls, and movies, producing the video hit, "I'm Bout It" and the motion picture release, *I Got the Hook Up*. .

None of these ventures, which had to be accompanied by an investment of time and money, would have been possible without these stars professing and projecting a "Professional Attitude." Each of them recognized the opportunities available and capitalized on them with the assistance of competent and experienced professional advisers. In the future, more entertainers and their advisers will have to be well-schooled (literally and figuratively) in several areas of expertise.

Besides grasping the fundamentals of developing and executing a business plan for each venture, one will need a variety of agreements detailing and clarifying each party's interest in each endeavor. As Judy Adams (widow of the late singer Johnny Adams) said in the acceptance speech for her husband's posthumous 1998 Heritage Award from the R&B Foundation, "Don't walk, run, [to] and get a good attorney." A professional attitude will be best displayed by the artists who get a good and experienced attorney, a competent accountant, and other knowledgeable business advisers.

A professional attitude will bring success and the success will be determined not only by the fame achieved, but also the fortune an artist (producer, artist, songwriter, etc.) is able to build for the future after acquiring such fame. I believe that success in the music business is not a myth or pipedream and it is still possible to build an empire based on available opportunities.

Artists like The Isleys (formerly the Isley Brothers) established celebrity status with their appearance in one of R. Kelly's videos and were catapulted into gold certification for their subsequently released CD; Diedre Hicks starred on Broadway in Smokey Joe's Cafe; and Toni Braxton and Debbie Gibson both starred as Beauty in the Broadway hit, "Beauty and the Beast." There is also the successful advent of artists of different genres who have recorded together in an effort to expand their fan base. You'll find that R. Kelly has teamed up with Celine Dion for the duet, "I'm Your Angel," while George Michael and Mary J. Blige released *As* and, prior to his passing, Frank Sinatra recorded a series of duet CDs with Anita Baker and Luther Vandross. Today, we also see many artists generally associated with one category of music recording material from other categories. They're "crossing over" to selling on different charts, recognizing that music is for the masses. Not only do we find that (after stepping in for Luciano Pavoratti) Aretha Franklin announced she is recording classical selections with the Detroit Symphony (subsequent to her R&B hit single, "A Rose Is Still A Rose," produced by hip-hop artist, Lauryn Hill) but also that Shirley Caesar has recorded a CD featuring certain classical selections. Yes! There are many and various ways to stay in business and the opportunities will be expanded even further in the future.

It is also important to know the market and that the types of music that are selling is rapidly changing. Whereas in the early to mid-1990s, pop rock and alternative rock were the big sellers, what were considered subgenres during that time—rap, hip-hop, country, and Latin music—are now the fastest-growing markets, with gospel music being introduced on the charts and in concert halls across the country in a whole new way.

## RAP & HIP-HOP

In 1998, rap music outsold country music. Interestingly enough, rap artists are among the leaders in the industry in adopting the proper perspective that you don't have to have a major label deal to sell significant amounts of product. A prime example is the success of rapper/entrepreneur, Master P, who started his business several years ago by selling his tapes from his own record store in California. Currently, he sells millions of records a year by several artists on his own No Limit Records label. His sales through independent distributor, Priority Records, was a major reason Priority was purchased by EMI distribution in the late 1990s. Rap and hip-hop are the new millenium's "Sound of Young America," a term coined by Motown in the 1960s.

Preparing for the future requires recognition of the tremendous melding of musical styles and cross-genre appeal of several types of music. You never really know who's listening to or who's buying your product. Gerald Levert is unjustifiably labeled by many as strictly an R&B star. But his *Love and Consequences* CD released two consecutive gold singles, earning him *Billboard* Pop Top Twenty chart status. Following his performance during the 1999 Grammy Awards, for example, former Menudo star and Latin singer Ricky Martin saw his album completely sold out in record stores in Salt Lake City, Utah (hardly a mecca for Latin music). Music moves around faster than we do and a piece of powerful product moves even faster than that, part of another movement people in the music business need to be mindful of—the "The Latin Connection."

## THE LATIN CONNECTION

One of the-fastest growing segments of the record industry is the Latin market. In 1998, sales in this genre grew by 21%. A decade after the initial domestic crossover, success of acts such as Gloria Estefan (on the heels of the death of Selena, who, at the time of her death was poised for the successful launch of her English-speaking debut CD) provide a whole new wave of Latin-based performers, who are ready to explode in the U.S. market. While major labels are finally taking this market seriously, there is still the potential for independent labels to make their mark. Ricky Martin's electrifying performance at the Grammy Awards signaled to the industry that Latin music is ready to capture the mainstream audience and acts like Marc Anthony, Jennifer Lopez, and others are leading the way. Well-written and produced material in this genre is bound to carve a significant slice out of the overall record market pie. The artists in this area of music will have to make sure they educate themselves and seek professional advice so that they, too, have an understanding of the evolving mechanics of the business.

## THE GOSPEL TRUTH

The RIAA has confirmed that gospel music's market share doubled from 1995 to 1998. Fueled by the massive crossover success of Kirk Franklin, this genre is proving to be another of the fastest-growing markets in the music business. Several of the major labels have purchased what used to be small, privately owned, gospel labels, and directed this genre's sales beyond the traditional religious bookstore retailers. Many of these traditional Christian bookstores have evolved into "superstores," increasing their floor space and product selections to include videos and other products aimed at its target market. Several other gospel artists, such as Fred Hammond and John P. Kee, have achieved gold or platinum certifications for their recent CDs. Not long after his double platinum success with the group God's Property, Kirk Franklin and his record company was hit with a lawsuit by the founder and alleged leader of the group, claiming she was cheated out of profits from the group's involvement with the CD. As the gospel market continues to grow, it will be even more important for musicians, singers, choir directors, and company owners to more fully understand the rights and obligations contained in contracts formerly used primarily for rock, country, and R&B acts that sell millions of CDs. Contracts dealing with the relationship of gospel acts can be particularly complicated. Issues such as the size of the choir; who should or should not perform at recording sessions and live performances; what, if any, royalty should be paid to the choir members; as well as the effect of donations of members performances for the benefit of nonprofit corporations or church entities, are all important matters which should be decided and reduced to writing to prevent disagreements should the act achieve the success of substantial record sales.

A proper perspective and professional attitude can assist artists, songwriters, producers, and record company executives who plan to stay in business. And as more artists branch out with their powerful product they'll recognize that what worked yesterday may not work the same way today to enable them to succeed in the future. But let's keep foremost in our minds that as professionals and creative people surviving in the record industry we've undertaken a broad endeavor and we have to recognize it is time—like no other—to Take Care of Your Music Business. And that's the gospel truth.

# Index